Bible Prophecy 101

An Overview Study of Bible Prophecy In Five Lessons

Bible Prophecy 101 - An Overview Study of Bible Prophecy In Five Lessons

Printed in the U.S.A.

ISBN-13:
978-1505843392
ISBN-10:
1505843391

Unless otherwise indicated, Bible quotations are taken from The King James Version.

www.maranathaevangelisticministries.com
email: al_gist@hotmail.com

Table of Contents

Bible Prophecy 101

An Overview Study of Bible Prophecy in Five Lessons

Introduction

The Bible teaches that these "last days" in which we live will be "perilous" (II Tim. 3:1). And it certainly goes without saying that socially, politically, economically and internationally, we are witnessing troublesome times on every side. However, for those who know Jesus Christ as their Savior and what His Word says about these last days, there is great comfort and security. We are not left in the dark about what to expect in these final days of the age and He promises that our welfare is His great concern. Through all the hardships that life may present, He will never leave us nor forsake us (Heb. 13:5). And soon… He will come to take us to our Heavenly Home!

Join us as we take this incredible journey through God's Word to discover what He has told us about these perilous last days in which we live. Bible Prophecy is NOT impossible to understand. God has given us His Prophetic Word to encourage us and inform us about what He is up to. He wants us to know about these last days because that knowledge brings great joy and peace in a time when true joy and peace are hard to find.

After the Apostle Paul described the Rapture of the Church in 1 Thessalonian 4, he said,

*"Wherefore **comfort** one another with these words."* (1 Thess. 4:18)

I pray that this short study of God's prophetic Word will comfort your heart and give you peace in these turbulent times and will increase your faith in the plan and power of God that He is working out through His Son, Jesus Christ.

Bible Prophecy 101

Lesson 1

The Rapture

We will begin our study on a topic that many will think is unpleasant… the topic of DEATH.

For the Christian, death is NOT to be feared, but should be seen as simply as a "transition" from this mortal world into a more perfect, eternal state… a state that will be full of joy, peace, and unimaginable happiness. But perhaps, the thing that makes the experience of physical death so fearful, like many other things, is the "unknown factor". People always fear the unknown. By nature, we are creatures of habit. We like routine. We like familiarity. We like living in an environment that we understand and can navigate in with calm assurance of the outcome.

But the unknown is fearful.

- Many fear exploring unexplored places for fear of not knowing what they may encounter…
- Some people are afraid of the dark because it hides things from them and they don't like "NOT KNOWING" what's in their surroundings…
- For most people, there is some degree of being uncomfortable when they're in a crowd of strangers, as oppose to the comfort we feel when we're surrounded by friends and family with whom we are familiar.

So, hopefully, this fear of death can be overcome (at least *partially*) by learning more about what to expect in that moment of "transition into the immortal state". Possessing a real confidence in the glorious future that awaits us beyond this mortal existence can allay our fears about the experience of getting there. And this study will help provide information from the infallible and inerrant Word of God (a perfectly accurate and true source of information) about what is in the future of all true born-again believers.

So, what does the Bible say about the experience of physical death? How does it define "death"?

The Bible teaches that there are two births and two deaths. We've all experienced that initial birth from our mother's womb into this world. But Jesus told Nicodemus that there is a second "spiritual birth" that takes place when a person realizes that he is a sinner and seeks forgiveness of his sins from God by placing his full faith in the fact that Jesus died FOR him in payment of his transgressions against God. At that moment of putting his faith in Jesus Christ and what He did for him, he is "born again". If you want to have eternal life with Christ, Jesus said to Nicodemus that "*Ye must be born again.*" (John 3:7) This is the Second Birth.

This won't necessarily prevent you from dying the first death (physical death), but it will definitely prevent you from dying the second death where all the unredeemed of the ages will be thrown into a Lake of Fire (Rev. 20:13-15)… a place of eternal torment.

So, we could say it this way…
There are two births and two deaths. If you are born only once, then you will die twice. But if you are born twice, you will only die once… and maybe not even once if Jesus comes for His Church first.

The first death, the physical death, is often misunderstood. Most people do not know what death is from a Biblical perspective.

Physical death is **temporary and reversible**. The reversal of physical death is what we call RESURRECTION.

On a grave from the 1880s in Nantucket, Massachusetts:

Under the sod and under the trees,
Lies the body of Jonathan Pease.
He is not here, there's only the pod.
Pease shelled out and went to God.

Though it's stated as a humorous pun, this epitaph makes a theologically sound statement, if Jonathan Pease was indeed a Christian. Physical death is nothing more than "shelling out of this old pod" (body). And the Bible teaches us that one day the "pod" will be re-inhabited (in the Resurrection)… although it will be a MUCH IMPROVED pod (body).

Man is a THREE-PART BEING...Body, Soul, and Spirit.
Gen. 1:27 - *"So God created man in His own image, in the image of God created He him; male and female created He them."*

As God Himself is a Triune Godhead... Father, Son, and Holy Spirit… so He created us as a three-part being… Body, Soul, and Spirit.
Gen. 2:7 - *"And the lord God formed man of the dust of the ground, and breathed into his nostrils the breath of life; and man BECAME A LIVING SOUL."*

This is what separates us from the animal world. In the creation of all the animals in nature, we have no record that God imparted a "soul" into any of them. Even though there may be some similarities to the way man lives, thinks, and acts, there is this one distinct difference between man and the animal kingdom… MAN HAS AN ETERNAL SOUL.

When Paul is concluding his letter to the Thessalonians, he says:
I Thess. 5:23 - *"And the very God of peace sanctify you wholly* [completely; entirely]; *and I pray God your whole spirit and soul and body be preserved blameless unto the coming of our Lord Jesus Christ."*

So, you and I are THREE-PART beings… body, soul, and spirit. When physical death occurs, there is a separation of the three parts. The soul and spirit depart from the body. As a born-again believer in Jesus Christ, the spirit and soul goes *immediately to Heaven* to be with Jesus. But because of sin, our earthly body goes to the grave and returns to the dust of this earth. Of course, at the death of an unbeliever, in his spiritual form, he goes to Hell (Luke 16:22-28).

God warned Adam against eating of the forbidden fruit:
Gen. 2:17 - *"...thou shalt not eat of it: for in the day that thou eatest thereof thou shalt surely die."*

This is a reference to both the **spiritual death** (eternal separation from God) because sin had entered into mankind and holy God cannot be in the presence of sin. But it also a reference to the **physical death** that would come as a result of man's sinful disobedience to God. We see this in the curse that God placed Adam (and mankind) when He said,

Gen. 3:19 - *"In the sweat of thy face shalt thou eat bread, till thou return unto the ground; for out of it wast thou taken; for dust thou art, and unto dust shalt thou return."*

It was the **physical body** of Adam that was formed out of the dust when God created him. So it was the **body** of Adam that returned to the dust when he died the physical death.

So, at death, the soul and spirit depart from the body and it (the body) goes back to the dust. But in one's *soulish form* (in soul and spirit), as a Christian, he immediately goes to Heaven to be with Jesus.

Now, some try to teach that upon death, we go into the grave as body, soul, and spirit in a kind of "soul sleep" and there we wait until the day of resurrection. But *that is not what the Bible teaches!*

2 Cor. 5:6 - *"Therefore we are always confident, knowing that, whilst we are at home in the body, we are absent from the Lord:*
7   (For we walk by faith, not by sight:)
8   We are confident, I say, and willing rather to be absent from the body, and to be present with the Lord."

So, for the Christian, *to be absent from the body, is to be present with the Lord!*

Jesus speaks to the thief on the cross

Do you remember what Jesus said to the thief on the cross? There were two thieves who were crucified with Jesus, one on either side of Him.

The Impenitent Thief railed against the Lord and said, *"If thou be Christ, then save yourself and us."* (Luke 23:39) However, the Penitent Thief said, *"Lord, remember me when thou comest into thy kingdom."* (Luke 23:42) Jesus told THAT man, *"Today shalt thou be with me in Paradise."* (Luke 23:43)

But that afternoon, Joseph of Arimathea and Nicodemus took the Lord's body off the cross and laid it in a borrowed tomb. So the skeptic might ask, "Where was He? In the tomb or in Paradise?"

He was in BOTH PLACES! About 3:00 in the afternoon, Jesus cried with a loud voice and said, *"Father, into thy hands I commend my spirit."* (Luke 23:46) and he *"gave up the ghost!"* (His spirit departed his body… *He died!*) At that point, He was DEAD. His body was put in the tomb, but in His spirit, He went to Paradise to meet with that penitent thief (and take care of some other business).

Then, on the third day, He re-entered that body and came forth from the grave ALIVE! It was His same body, but it was different for it was now a glorified body. Jesus then went to His disciples who were cowering in fear of the Jewish leaders in a closed room (John 20:26) and the Bible says that He just appeared in their midst. So then, in His glorified state, Jesus had supernatural powers that His earthly body did not possess… like the ability to simply pass right through walls and doors. Obviously, in that sense, His body was *different.*

But nevertheless, it was that same body that hung on the cross because:
- He showed them the scars in His hands and side.
- He told Thomas to put his finger into the wound in His side where that Roman soldier had thrust Him through with a spear.
- He asked them for some food and ate some fish and honeycomb in front of them… NOT because He was hungry, but because He wanted to show them that He was not just some apparition. He was real… with a tangible body.

He had re-entered that same body and was now ALIVE! We call this the Resurrection. It is the reversal of Death. At death, the soul and spirit separate from the body. And, in the resurrection, the soul and spirit re-enter the body and the person becomes alive again.

Jesus came forth from the grave, victorious over death, and by doing so, became the Firstfruit of a much greater harvest of people who will do the same thing.

He set the example:
I Cor. 15:22-24b - *"For as in Adam all die* [ever since the sin of Adam, people have had to suffer death], *even so in Christ shall all be made alive. But every man in his own order:* **Christ the first fruits***; afterward they that are Christ's at His coming. Then cometh the end..."*

Every child of God who dies today and goes to Heaven, is DEAD. But the day is coming when they will receive new resurrected bodies AT the Rapture of the Church. They will get a new, glorified body and they'll be ALIVE.

If people are happy in Heaven just as they are (spirit and soul), then why is it important for them to come back and receive a new body? Because NOW they are dead, but Jesus promised them (those who are saved) **eternal life!** (John 3:16).

So, the day will come (AT the Rapture) when the Lord will descend to the atmosphere of our planet. Along with Him, will come the spirits and souls of all Christians who will have died up to that point. There will be a trumpet blast and new, glorified bodies will be resurrected to join with the souls and spirits of those dead saints, making them once again a three-part being... ALIVE.

This is called The First Resurrection and it will happen at the time of the Rapture. We want to talk about it, but first, to avoid confusion, let me make it clear that there are at least Three TYPES of Resurrection mentioned in the Scriptures:

1. National Resurrection - As when Israel was dead and buried in the Gentile nations of the world, but now has been brought back to national life. (Hosea 6:1-2)
2. Spiritual Resurrection - Takes place when a person is born again. He goes from being dead in his trespasses and sin to being spiritually alive.

3. Physical Resurrection - The literal, bodily resurrection from the grave... going from a state of death back to the state of being alive again.

Of course, we are focusing on the phenomenon of PHYSICAL RESURRECTION.

So, I say again...
The FIRST RESURRECTION is the resurrection of the Righteous who will live and reign with Christ during the 1000 year Millennial Kingdom. And the Bible says that the SECOND DEATH does NOT have power over them (Rev. 20:6). In other words, they will not suffer the Second Death.

The Second Death is for the WICKED DEAD who will be resurrected in the SECOND RESURRECTION. We'll discuss it a little more in just in minute. But for now... Let's talk about the FIRST RESURRECTION, which is the resurrection of the Righteous (those who have put their faith in Jesus Christ).

The First Resurrection is actually in THREE PHASES. This is indicated in

1 Cor. 15:20 - *"But now is Christ risen from the dead, and become the firstfruits of them that slept.*
21   For since by man [Adam] came death [physical death], by man [Jesus] came also the resurrection of the dead.
22   For as in Adam all die, even so in Christ shall all be made alive.
23   But every man in his own order: Christ the firstfruits; afterward they that are Christ's at his coming.
24   Then cometh the end..."

The word that is translated here as "order" is the Greek "tagma" and it is a military term that means "an orderly arrangement... like a band, brigade, or group". In other words, Paul was saying that every person will be resurrected *in his own group*.

And the first phase (or group) in the First Resurrection is the:

1.   The Resurrection of the FIRST FRUITS

The Resurrection of the First Fruits took place almost two thousand years ago. As we've already discussed, Jesus became THE First Fruit of the Resurrection. He set the example. Had He not been victorious over death and the grave, what hope would we have that WE could be resurrected unto everlasting life?

So JESUS was absolutely the FIRST to be resurrected unto eternal life. But you say, "What about Lazarus and others that Jesus resurrected?"

Well, those people all eventually died again. But Jesus came forth from the grave ALIVE forever more. He told John on the Isle of Patmos, some 47 years after His death, burial, and resurrection:
Rev. 1:18a - *"I am he that liveth, and was dead; and, behold, **I am alive for evermore**, Amen..."*

However, the Bible also tells us in Matthew 27 that immediately AFTER Jesus was resurrected, many of the OT saints were also resurrected.
Matt 27:52 - *"And the graves were opened; and many bodies of the saints which slept arose,*
53   And came out of the graves after his resurrection, and went into the holy city, and appeared unto many."

So, even though Jesus is THE First Fruit of the Resurrection, there were also some OT saints who were resurrected at that time (right AFTER Him). And although the Bible doesn't say so specifically, we would have to assume that He took those saints to Heaven with Him in their new resurrected bodies and they are there now in that state.

Now, the second phase of the First Resurrection is what we might call…

2.   The MAIN PART of the Resurrection

And, we can call it that because, without a doubt, the largest number of people in the First Resurrection will be resurrected at that time.

Notice again what it says in

1 Cor. 15:23 - *"But every man in his own order: Christ the firstfruits;* [That's the first phase] *afterward they that are Christ's at his coming.* [That's the second phase... the time of the MAIN RESURRECTION] *"* And this is talking about His coming for the Church at the Rapture... NOT His Second coming.

And then, the third phase of the First Resurrection will be...

3.   The GLEANINGS of the Resurrection

These are those saints who die DURING the Tribulation. At the end of the Tribulation, when Jesus will come in great power and glory at His Second Coming, He will resurrect those who died for Him during the Tribulation.

In Rev. 20:4 it says, *"...and I saw them that were beheaded* **[DEAD!]** *for the witness of Jesus, and for the word of God, and which had not worshiped the beast, neither his image, neither had received his mark upon their foreheads, or in their hands;* **and they lived** *and reigned with Christ a thousand years."*

John saw those who had died for Christ during the Tribulation and they were ALIVE again. That is, they had been resurrected. Since they died DURING the Tribulation and John sees them ALIVE and reigning with Christ during the 1000 year Millennial Kingdom that follows, they MUST have been resurrected at the Second Coming of the Lord.

So, the First Resurrection, which is the resurrection of the saints of God, is marked in three phases...

1. The First Fruits (Jesus and some of the OT saints),
2. The Main Harvest (at the Rapture when all the *"dead in Christ"* shall rise), and
3. The Gleanings of the harvest (the Tribulation saints at the Second Coming).

But there is also to be a harvest of the *"tares"*...

Rev. 20:6 says, *"Blessed and holy is he that hath part in the first resurrection* [Why? Because that is the resurrection of the believers]*: on such the second death hath no power, but they shall be priests of God and of Christ, and shall reign with him a thousand years* [during the Millennial Kingdom].*"*

But verse 5 says, *"But the rest of the dead* [which would be all the unbelievers] *lived not again **until** the thousand years were finished."* The clear implication is that the unbelievers will **live** again at the end of the thousand years.

At the end of the thousand year Millennial Kingdom, God will then cause the Second Resurrection to take place. Since all **believers** will have been resurrected in the First Resurrection, that means the Second Resurrection will be for all *unbelievers*. They will be resurrected back to life to stand before God's Great White Throne and be judged.

Now, remember…
What happens to a **lost** person when they die? Their body goes to the grave. But their soul and spirit go to Hell… the very place where the "rich man" is STILL being tormented in its flames (Luke 16:23).

All people will be resurrected back to life… eventually. Many people don't understand that everyone, both saved and unsaved, will be resurrected… *"some to everlasting life, and some to everlasting shame and contempt."* (Dan. 12:2) Some *"unto the resurrection of life"* and some *"unto the resurrection of damnation"* (John 5:28-29). Acts 24:15 says there is *"a resurrection of the dead, both of the just and the unjust".*

The saved will all be resurrected in what the Bible calls "The First Resurrection" and will not die the second death, but will reign with Christ in His earthly Millennial Kingdom (Rev. 20:6) and spend eternity with Him (I Thess. 4:17-18).
Rev. 20:6 – *"Blessed and holy is he that hath part in the first resurrection."*

So, let's now read about the Second Resurrection (the resurrection of the Unrighteous) from Hell in Rev. 20:11 where John says,

11   *"And I saw a great white throne,* [This is what we refer to as The Great White Throne Judgment of God. And it will happen AFTER the 1000 year Millennial Kingdom.] *and him that sat on it, from whose face the earth and the heaven fled away; and there was found no place for them.*

12   *And I saw the dead, small and great, stand before God;* [Now, remember WHO are the dead that he's talking about? Those who exist without a body in that "soulish state". At this point in time, it COULD NOT refer to the Righteous Dead because all of them will have been already resurrected in the First Resurrection. And we'll see in a moment that these are the REST of the dead... i.e. the Unrighteous Dead.] *and the books were opened: and another book was opened, which is the book of life: and the dead were judged out of those things which were written in the books, according to their works.* [So, these people are judged according to their works... or deeds]

13   *And the sea gave up the dead which were in it; and death* [This is a reference to the GRAVE] *and hell* [This is the place where the wicked dead, in their soulish state are NOW being held. It is a place of terrible torment.] *delivered up the dead which were in them: and they were judged every man according to their works.*

14   *And death and hell were cast into the lake of fire.* [Literally, those who came up from "death and hell" or "the grave and hell"] *This is the second death.*

15   *And whosoever was not found written in the book of life was cast into the lake of fire."*

The "Lake of Fire" is NOT Hell. Hell is the place where unsaved people go NOW. But we just read that they will be resurrected out of Hell to stand ALIVE in front of God's Great White Throne of judgment.

And then, because their names are NOT found written in "book of life", they are cast ALIVE into the Lake of Fire… that eternal place of torment and suffering. It's the place that was prepared by God for the Devil and His angels. And, if you'll look back at vs. 10, you'll see that it is the place where God sends old Satan to suffer forever.

So, when a person is cast alive into the Lake of Fire, the Bible says THIS is the second death. Now, you can't die if you're not alive. So, the wicked dead are resurrected back to life for just long enough to be judged and thrown into the Lake of Fire, which annihilates the body…. eliminating all hopes of ever being alive again. In that incomplete, soulish state, they will suffer the pangs of fiery torment forever. This is the SECOND DEATH! It is eternal (Rev. 14:9-11) and irreversible.

Paul tells us in I Cor. 15:24-26, that in the end, Jesus *"shall have put down all rule and all authority and power. For he must reign, till he hath put all enemies under his feet. The last enemy that shall be destroyed is death."*

Through the resurrection of His saints unto everlasting life and through the ultimate and final destruction of death and hell at God's Great White Throne Judgment, Jesus will destroy the final enemy… DEATH!

Review of the Resurrections

So, let's review what we've said about the Resurrections.

1.   There are three TYPES of resurrections mentioned in the Bible:
1. National Resurrection – the resurrection of a people into a nation again (like Israel).
2. Spiritual Resurrection – when a person is saved, he goes from being dead in his trespasses and sin to being spiritually alive.
3. Physical Resurrection – a literal resurrection of the body from the grave and reuniting it with the soul and spirit. It is the reversal of physical death in which people are brought back to life.

2. **There will be TWO Physical Resurrections:**
The First Resurrection (of the Righteous)
The Second Resurrection (of the Unrighteous)

3. **The FIRST Resurrection will be in three phases:**
1. The Resurrection of the First Fruits (Of whom Jesus was the first)
2. The Main Resurrection (at the time of the Rapture)
3. The Resurrection of the Gleanings (the Tribulation Saints)

4. **The Second Resurrection is the resurrection of all people throughout the ages who have rejected Jesus and His offer of salvation.** They will be resurrected back to life to stand before the Great White Throne Judgment of God and be judged according to their wicked deeds. And because their names are NOT found written in the Lamb's Book of Life, they will be thrown into the everlasting Lake of Fire. This is the Second Death.

But let us return now to our discussion on The First Resurrection at the time the Main Part will be resurrected at the time of the Rapture.

The Main Harvest will take place when God, the Father, will look at His Son (His Only Begotten Son, Jesus) and will say, "Son, go get your bride." And the great archangel will cause the heavens to reverberate with a mighty, thunderous roar. And, Jesus will descend into the atmosphere of this planet with the spirits of those Christians who have already died.

There will be an ear-piercing trumpet blast and new, glorified bodies of those saints who have already died will ascend up, out of the ground, uniting with their souls and spirits.

There will be another trumpet blast, and then, those of us believers who are still alive at that point will be suddenly changed into our glorified bodies and we will ascend into the sky to meet the Lord.
THIS IS CALLED THE RAPTURE OF THE CHURCH.

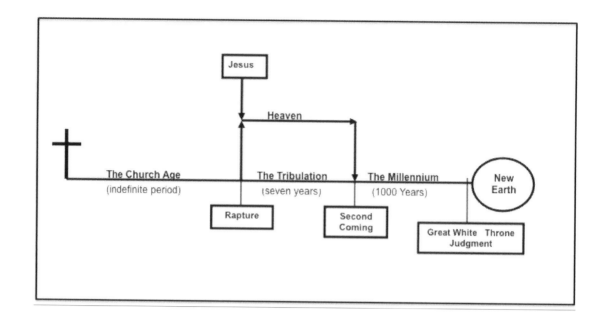

Distinguishing between the Rapture and the Second Coming

Now, some may say, "But isn't the Rapture the same thing as the Second Coming of Jesus?"

No. Actually, these are two different events, separated by at least seven years in time. But a lot of confusion comes from those who do not recognize them as two distinct events.

In the Rapture, Jesus does not come all the way to the earth. He only descends to the atmosphere and calls us up to Him. We read in

1 Thess. 4:16 - *"For the Lord himself shall descend from heaven with a shout, with the voice of the archangel, and with the trump of God: and the dead in Christ shall rise first:*
17 *Then we which are alive and remain shall be caught up together with them in the clouds, to meet the Lord in the air:"*

Also, Jesus said in
John 14:3 - *"And if I go and prepare a place for you, I will come again, and* **_receive_** *you unto myself; that where I am, there ye may be also."*

So, when the Lord comes for us in the Rapture, He will only come to the atmosphere and we will meet Him in the air, where He will RECEIVE us!

But at His glorious Second Coming, He will come all the way TO the earth. According Acts 1:11 and Zech. 14:4, He will set His feet down on the Mount of Olives, the very same place from which He ascended into Heaven.

In Acts 1, Jesus' disciples were told that that same Jesus Whom they had just watched ascend into Heaven would come back in like manner.

And Zech. 14:4 where it's talking about His glorious Second Coming, says, *"And His feet shall stand in that day upon the mount of Olives, which is before Jerusalem on the east…"*

In the Rapture…. Jesus will come FOR His saints.
In the Second Coming… Jesus will WITH His saints. (And there are many Scriptures that speak of Jesus coming *with* His saints. Zech. 14:5, Col. 3:4, 1Thess. 3:13, Jude 14)
But doesn't it make sense that He can't come WITH His saints until He first comes FOR His saints?

Pre-Trib. Position

But this brings us to another very important question concerning the Rapture of the Church…
How do we know that the Rapture will happen BEFORE the Tribulation begins?

There is a lot of debate about the TIMING of the Rapture…

1.   I'm convinced that the Bible teaches a *Pre-Tribulational Rapture…* that the Lord will come for His Bride BEFORE the Tribulation begins. And I'll give you the Scriptural support for this in just a moment…

2.   But, some say that it will happen at the end of the Tribulation and they connect it to the Second Coming. I call this the "Yo-yo" theory because they say the Lord will Rapture us up and then we will immediately come right back down with Him. They also believe, of course, that the Church must go through the seven years of Tribulation.

3.   And some can't seem to make up their mind about whether it will happen before or after the Tribulation, so they say that we'll be Raptured at the Mid-Point of the Tribulation.

Now, I'm not going to spend a lot of time trying to DISPROVE the other two views. But I DO want to give you some reasons for believing in a Pre-Tribulation Rapture.

Four Reasons to Believe in a Pre-Tribulation Rapture

Allow me to give you a BRIEF explanation of just FOUR REASONS I believe in a Pre-Tribulational Rapture:

1.   The Tribulation is the TIME OF GOD'S WRATH.
If there is one prevailing characteristic of that terrible time that we know as The Tribulation, it is that it is a time of God's WRATH. Unlike any other time in all of history, God will show His wrath against the ungodliness of mankind. Revelation 6:15-17 describes it this way:

Rev. 6:15 - *"And the kings of the earth, and the great men, and the rich men, and the chief captains, and the mighty men, and every bondman, and every free man, hid themselves in the dens and in the rocks of the mountains;*
16   And said to the mountains and rocks, Fall on us, and hide us from the face of him that sitteth on the throne, and from the wrath of the Lamb:
17   For the great day of his wrath is come; and who shall be able to stand?"

Without a doubt, the Tribulation will be the *"great day of His wrath"*. Not only will God remove His gracious ministry of restraining evil, that presently works through The Holy Spirit (II Thess. 2:6-7) so that crime, hatred, and cruelty will be at an all-time high, but He will also pour out unbelievable plagues upon humanity that will make life on earth nearly unbearable.

In fact, Jesus said that *"then shall be great tribulation, such as was not since the beginning of the world to this time, no , nor ever shall be. And except those days should be shortened, there should no flesh be saved:"* (Matt. 24:21:22a) Think of that! It will be a time *unparalleled* in all of history for its pain, heartache, and suffering! *It will be the day of God's wrath!*

But... the Bible declares that we, as **Christians, have been saved from that day of wrath**. Paul praised the church in Thessalonica for how they had *"turned to God from idols to serve the living and true God; And to wait for his Son from heaven, whom he raised from the dead, even Jesus which **delivered us from the wrath to come**."* (I Thess. 1:9b-10)

Notice that the verb "delivered" is past tense. *When* did Jesus deliver us from the wrath to come? The very moment we accepted Him as our savior! At that time, we became a part of the bride of Christ that will be taken from this earth at the end of the Church Age and **prior to** that day of great tribulation.

Paul makes that clear again in I Thess. 5:9 where he says, *"For God hath not appointed us* [us Christians] *to wrath, but to obtain salvation by our Lord Jesus Christ."*

Our salvation does not just save us from an eternal Hell, but also from that day of God's wrath...
*"But God commendeth His love toward us, in that, while we were yet sinners, Christ died for us. Much more then, being now justified by his blood, we **shall be saved** from wrath through Him."* (Romans 5:8-8) In other words, even more sure than our justification by His blood is our salvation from wrath through Him.

John declares that wrath is NOT for those who have put their trust in Jesus as the Son of God, but for those who do NOT trust in Jesus…

John 3:36 - *"He that believeth on the Son hath everlasting life: and he that believeth not the Son shall not see life; but the wrath of God abideth on him."*

Luke described the horrors of the Tribulation as the day when there will be *"distress of nations, with perplexity"* and *"men's hearts failing them for fear, and for looking after those things which are coming on the earth"* (Luke 21:25-26)

Then, he goes on to exhort his readers to:

Luke 21:36 - *"Watch ye therefore, and pray always, that ye may be accounted worthy to escape all these things that shall come to pass, and to stand before the Son of Man."* After the Church is taken from this world in the Rapture, we will stand before the Lord in the "Bema Judgment" while earth is going through The Tribulation (I Cor. 3:11-15, Rom. 14:12).

Pre-Wrath

Now, I know that there are some who claim that it is only in the second half of the Tribulation that God will pour out His wrath on humanity. And, so they've come up with the idea of a Mid-Trib. Rapture that will precede the last 3 ½ years, which we normally refer to as the day of GREAT Tribulation.

Many events of the whole seven years of the Tribulation are described for us beginning in Revelation 6 with the breaking of the first four of the seven Seal Judgments. These first four judgments bring on what we usually refer to as The Four Horsemen of the Apocalypse, each symbolic of four stages of suffering that this planet will go through _throughout the seven years_.

The first horseman rides a WHITE horse and he is symbolic of the Antichrist who *"goes forth conquering, and to conquer."* (Rev. 6:2)

The second horseman rides a RED horse, symbolic of the bloodshed of worldwide war. (Rev. 6:4)

The third horseman rides a BLACK horse, and he is symbolic of famine and starvation… which is the natural result of war. (Rev. 6:5-6)

The fourth horseman rides a PALE horse and the word that is translated as "pale" refers to a sickly, yellowish-green color that accompanies the dead and dying. Thus, this fourth horse represents massive death from the warring, the famine, and diseases that engulf the earth… resulting in the death of ¼ of the human population. (Rev. 6:8)

So, all four of these apocalyptic horsemen introduce the planet to the Antichrist, and worldwide war, famine, disease, and death. This is an overview of the horrors of the whole Seven Years of Tribulation. The whole seven years is the Daniel's 70th week… not just the last 3 ½ years of it!

The whole seven years is the "time of Jacob's trouble" (Jer. 30:7)
And the whole seven years is the day of God's wrath.

So, actually God's wrath begins with the rise of Antichrist and the associated war and bloodshed that starts Rev. 6. And THAT'S preceded by chapter 5 which gives us a picture of the Throne Room of God. And THAT is preceded by chapter four which begins with the door of Heaven being opened up and John hearing a voice saying, "Come up hither"… which, undoubtedly is symbolic of the Rapture. So, looking at it chronologically… the Rapture is pictured in chapter four and THEN in chapter 6, the wrath of the seven years of Tribulation begin.

Because remember…. The Church is described in detail in chapters 2&3, but we don't see any mention of her again until chapter 19, at the end of the Tribulation just before we return with the Lord Jesus in His glorious Second Coming.

So, for those who say that the WRATH of God doesn't begin until the second half of the Tribulation and the Church is raptured just before that, at the Mid-Point, just don't have an accurate view of the whole seven years.

And then, there are some who want to place the Rapture *at the end* of the Tribulation. Somehow, they see us going up in the Rapture and then returning immediately with the Lord in His Second Coming. But, there is a great deal of…

2. Difference between the Rapture and the Second Coming.

When one compares the I Thess. 4:13-18 (the description of the Rapture) with Revelation 19:11-21 (the description of the Second Coming), many differences are noted that indicate clearly that these are two separate events. For instance…

In the Rapture, we find Jesus coming FOR His saints. In the Second Coming, He comes back to earth WITH His saints.

In the Rapture, Jesus appears in the Heavens and we meet Him in the air. But in the Second Coming, Jesus puts His feet down on earth (Zech. 14:4) on the Mount of Olives, the place from which He ascended into Heaven (Acts 1:9-12).

In the Rapture, our Lord comes to claim the righteous. But in the Second Coming, He comes to condemn the unrighteous.

The whole nature of the two events is different! In the Rapture, Jesus is coming as our Savior to take us away to Heaven. So, Paul concludes his discussion on the Rapture by saying…
1 Thess 4:18 - *"Wherefore comfort one another with these words."*
The promise of the Rapture is a great COMFORT for God's children!

But in the Second Coming, Jesus will be returning as the King of Kings and the Lord of Lords…. Riding a white stallion… speaking destruction upon the enemies of God with the Sword of His Mouth… calling together the vultures and wild beasts to devour the rotting flesh of those who dared to stand against Him.

Do you see how DIFFERENT these two events are? They cannot be one in the same!

3.   Anything but a pre-trib Rapture destroys the doctrine of Imminence.

One of the most important doctrines of the Bible for the Church is the Doctrine of Imminence. Over and over again we are commanded to be ever watchful for our Lord's imminent coming. For instance, Jesus Himself said in
Matt. 24:42 - *"Watch therefore: for ye know not what hour your Lord doth come."*

And Mark says our Lord said it repeatedly in
Mark 13:33 - *"Take ye heed, **watch** and pray: for ye know not when the time is.*
*34   For the Son of man is as a man taking a far journey, who left his house, and gave authority to his servants, and to every man his work, and commanded the porter to **watch.***
*35   **Watch** ye therefore: for ye know not when the master of the house cometh, at even, or at midnight, or at the cockcrowing, or in the morning:*
36   Lest coming suddenly he find you sleeping.
*And what I say unto you I say unto all, **Watch**."*

The NT word that is translated here as "watch", carries with it the idea of vigilance. In other words, we are to be vigilant in our continual looking for our Lord's coming.

In theological circles, we like to call this the Doctrine of Immanency.

It states that Jesus could come for His people at any moment. There are no unfulfilled signs that must be fulfilled before Jesus comes for His Church. There are no uncompleted tasks that must be accomplished before He comes. There is no reason period that Jesus couldn't come tonight!

In fact, the "Doctrine of Immanency" is not only the idea that Jesus *could* come at any moment, but it is the belief that it looks like Jesus' coming *will be* at any moment.

David Brickner - "Many Christians are *waiting* for Christ's return, but few are *watching.* They've left the porch light on, but they have gone on to bed."

Our Lord describes as an *evil servant* the one who says to himself about his master who has gone away, *"My Lord delayeth his coming..."* (Matt. 24:24:48). Here is one who has the attitude that his master is not going to return anytime soon, so he begins to *"smite his fellow servants, and to eat and drink with the drunken".* In other words, without that sense of his master's imminent return in his heart, he begins to live very worldly, in a manner that is not pleasing to his lord.

So, Jesus went on to say that the lord of that evil servant *"will come in a day when he looketh not for him, and in an hour that he is not aware of. And shall cut him asunder..."* (Matt. 24:50-51)

Obviously, if the Rapture is to occur at the mid-point or at the end of the Tribulation, then any good Bible student would be able to mark the beginning of the seven year tribulation and calculate to the day when the Rapture would come.

If the Rapture must happen AFTER the Tribulation starts, then instead of watching for the Christ, we should be looking for the Antichrist! But we are never commanded in the Bible to look for the Antichrist. We are told repeatedly to watch for the return of Jesus Christ.

But because Jesus will come for His Church AFTER the Church Age is completed when the last soul has been added to the body and BEFORE the Tribulation begins, no one knows when that moment will be. Hence, we are commanded to be always watching for His imminent return.

4.   The Tribulation is not about the Church.

One of the most common mistakes about the Tribulation is not understanding what it is and who it is about. It is the seventieth week of years (7 years) that God told Daniel that He was going to deal with Daniel's people (the Jews). While the prophet is praying, God sends the angel Gabriel with a message for Daniel in which He says

Dan. 9:24 - *"Seventy weeks are determined upon thy people and upon thy holy city, to finish the transgression, and to make an end of sins, and to make reconciliation for iniquity, and to bring in everlasting righteousness, and to seal up the vision and prophecy, and to anoint the most Holy."*

We don't have time here to discuss the six reasons listed for the Tribulation period, but basically it is a time determined by God upon Daniel's people, the Jews. Although all the people who are still in the world (Jews and Gentiles) will suffer during that terrible time, it is primarily an earthly judgment upon the Jewish people in which God will bring their transgressions and sins to an end and bring in everlasting righteousness. This is why the Tribulation is often referred to as "Daniel's Seventieth Week".

Jeremiah calls it *"the time of Jacob's trouble"* (Jer. 30:7). You will remember that Jacob's name was changed to Israel. It will be the time of Israel's trouble!

The Tribulation is not about the Church!

Some have stated that the Church must go through part or all of the Tribulation in order to be **purified.** However, it is not tribulation that purifies the Church. It is the blood of Jesus that washes us clean. Like the old hymn says… "What can wash away my sin? **Nothing** but the blood of Jesus."

To indicate that our suffering will somehow cleanse us and make us fit as the bride of Jesus is to say that our Lord's work on the cross was insufficient in accomplishing that… that something MORE is required to get us ready for His presence. Of course, nothing could be farther from the truth! As the writer of Hebrews states,
Heb. 10:14 - *"For by one offering* [His death on the cross] *he* [Jesus] *hath perfected forever them that are sanctified."*

The idea of the Bride of Christ suffering in order to be prepared to meet her Groom is utter nonsense. Since when does the Groom feel that He must first inflict suffering upon his bride in order to prepare her for himself. Our Lord is NOT such a sadist Who wants to inflict pain upon the one He loves and gave Himself for!

The truth is, the Tribulation is not ABOUT the Church! It is not FOR the Church! In fact, it has nothing at all to do with the Church!

When the last person has been born into God's Kingdom and the Church, the Bride of Christ is complete, Jesus will come for His Bride and take us to a place that He is presently preparing for us (John 14:2). There, we will enjoy the great Marriage Feast of the Lamb while the world below is going through the worst seven years of tribulation it will ever experience!

Picture Types of the Pre-Tribulation Rapture

Now, I want to caution you that we must be careful not to build our doctrines based upon "Picture Types" in the Bible. But it is very interesting how that once we've established our doctrinal beliefs upon solid Scriptural evidence, we can see "Picture Types" in the OT that illustrate those very same truths. For example…

Joseph is a picture type of our Lord Jesus:
- You will remember how Joseph came to his brothers with a revelation from God, but they would not receive it.
- Joseph was thrown into a pit by his brothers… but he did not stay there. He came up out of the pit. This is a picture of the death, burial, and resurrection of Jesus.
- Joseph went away and married a Gentile bride (her name was Asenath) during the time that he was rejected by his brethren and BEFORE the famine came (a picture of The Tribulation, because it was a time of judgment on his brethren.) Jesus is today "taking a bride from among the Gentiles" BEFORE the Tribulation begins.

Moses is also picture type of Christ:
- He also married a Gentile bride… AFTER his rejection by his brethren, but BEFORE they passed through the tribulation put on them by Pharoah.

Enoch is a picture of the "Translation Saints".
- He was caught out BEFORE the Flood (a type of the Tribulation), but Noah and his family (a type of the Jewish remnant) were saved through the flood.

The word "Rapture"
Now, even though the word "Rapture" is not found in the pages of the Bible, it is a word that means "caught out" or "snatched away". And, it is a good word to describe this blessed event when Jesus comes to get His people.

He said, *"I go to prepare a place for you and if I go and prepare a place for you, I will come again and RECEIVE you unto myself, that where I am, there you may be also."*

So, Friend…
Without a doubt…
The next great event in the history of the Church is the Rapture.
Soon, the trumpet will sound and in an instant, we'll be snatched away to meet our Lord in the air.

Now, let's talk about exactly *HOW* the Rapture is going to happen:

I Thess. 4:13-18
Background on I Thessalonians:
The Apostle Paul made his first missionary journey through the area of Asia minor (Turkey) preaching the Gospel and establishing churches. And, in that mission trip, Paul took a dear friend with him named Barnabas, and another young fellow named John Mark.

Not too far into the trip, John Mark abandoned the group and returned to Jerusalem. (we don't know why), but Paul and Barnabas completed their missionary journey and returned to Antioch.

Some time later, Paul feels led of the Spirit to return to those churches they had established on his first missionary journey. So, he tells Barnabas about it and Barnabas says, "Fine. I'll go get John Mark and we'll get ready to go." But Paul says, "Wait a minute Barnabas, John Mark's not going with us." Barnabas says, "Oh yes he is." Paul says, "No, he isn't." And the Bible says the *contention* between them over this issue was so sharp, that they split up and went their separate ways.

Barnabas took John Mark (his nephew, Col. 4:10) and sailed off to Cyprus (the direction they had gone in their first trip). But Paul chose Silas, and went NW on foot revisiting the churches in that area....
Derbe, and Lystra, where he met a young man named Timothy, who joined them.

The Bible says that they were forbidden of the Holy Spirit to go eastward into Asia....
They *"assayed to go into Bithynia, but the Spirit suffered them not."* (Acts 16:7). So they went westward down to the little coastal town of Troas. And, it was there that the Apostle Paul had a vision of a man in Macedonia, saying, *"Come over into Macedonia and help us."* (Acts 16:9)

Understanding this to be a message from God, they boarded a ship and sailed over to Macedonia (northern Greece)... went through Samothacia, Neapolis, to Philipi. It was here that they were beaten, thrown into jail, and the Philippian jailer was converted.

After they were released, they went to Thessalonica. And even though their message was well received, there were some Jews there who began to persecute them. We call them the "Judaizers"... Jews who were committed to keeping every letter of the Law in order to find favor with God. But here comes Paul, preaching that the only way that a person can be accepted by God is by putting his faith in what this man Jesus did for him in Jerusalem a few years ago and that our efforts at observing the Law will never be good enough to get us into Heaven.

Well, these Judaizers thought Paul was a heretic, teaching false doctrine, and they hated him for it. So much so, that they were about to KILL Paul, so he had to leave town after being there for only three sabbath days (3 weeks).

From there, they went to Berea and the people there were *even more* receptive to the Gospel message.

But when the Judaizers in Thessalonica heard about what was going on in Berea, they went down there and stirred up a mob against Paul. So, once again... he had to leave town. The brethren put him on a ship and he sailed down to Athens, but he left Silas and Timothy in Berea.

Now, it appears that possibly Paul instructed his missionary partners to go back and check on the young church at Thessalonica. Because he sailed to Athens, stayed there a while... preached on Mars Hill... And then went over to Corinth, where he stayed for a year and a half.

It was while he was at Corinth that Silas and Timothy caught up with him and reported on the condition of the church at Thessalonica. Then, Paul, led of the Holy Spirit, sat down and penned to the church in Thessalonica what most scholars believe is his earliest writing in the Bible... the book of I Thessalonians.

It seems that this infant church, where Paul had only had three weeks to establish them in the faith and doctrine, was confused about several things.... but especially about the doctrines of end time events. From the letter that Paul wrote, it seems that some of the new Christians (who probably came out of Judaism) still had some of that Jewish thinking that was confusing them.

The Jewish thought about the Messiah (and they still think this today) was that the day would come when the Messiah will come and establish His Kingdom over all the earth and Israel as the head of all nations. Now that IS going to happen. This is the major theme of the OT prophets. One day, Jesus will come back to earth... defeat the enemies of God... and establish His kingdom on earth where He will rule in peace, justice, and righteousness for 1000 years. This is what we call the Millennial Kingdom.

But those Thessalonian Jewish Christians began to wonder, "But what about my loved ones, who died as Christians. If they're already DEAD, how are they going to participate in The Kingdom?"

So we find Paul explaining the Rapture (which will also include the Resurrection) in chapter 4:

I Thess. 4:13 - *"But I would not have you to be ignorant, brethren,* This comprises a large part of the Church today... the "Ignorant Brethren"... meaning "unknowledgeable".

"...concerning them which are asleep..."
"asleep" is a reference to physical death. Even as sleep is a temporary state, so the physical death of the body is a temporary, and reversible state.

"...that you sorrow not, even as others which have no hope..."
Be assured... There are many *others which have no hope!* When people are living their lives without a personal knowledge of and communion with Jesus Christ, they have no hope! For them, Death is the ultimate enemy! It is the final curtain... the ultimate end. And when they lose someone to death, they sink in absolute despair because to them, they have reached the end. There is no hope for a new life... a better tomorrow. They know nothing of the joys of Heaven, of the beautiful eternal glories that await The Redeemed! It's just The End.

Oh! But for us who know the Lord Jesus.... *"eye hath not seen, nor ear heard, neither have entered into the heart of men, what God has prepared for them that love Him."* (I Cor. 2:9)
We have not even *imagined* the beauties, and the peace, and the joy that God has in store for us!

14. *"For if we believe...."*
"if" could also be translated with the preposition "since"
"For [since] *we believe that Jesus died and rose again,..."*
And *this is* what we believe... Is it not?

"...even so [i.e., in just the same way] *them also which sleep in Jesus will God bring with him."*

That is, in the same way that Jesus Who is the Firstfruit of a much greater Harvest... In the same way that He came forth from the grave in victory over death.... In that same way, those who "sleep in Jesus", i.e. those Christians who have already died... will God bring with Him when He comes!

"If [since] *we believe that Jesus died and rose again, even so* [just the same way] *them also which sleep in Jesus* [dead Christians] *will God bring with Him."*

15. *For this we say unto you by the word of the Lord, that we which are alive and remain unto the coming of the Lord shall not prevent* [precede] *them which are asleep.*
You see, the Thessalonians were concerned that their loved ones who had already died were going to miss out on the glorious coming of the Messiah. But Paul told them "NOT so!" They're actually going to meet the Lord before we do (those of us who are living at the time of the Rapture).

16. *For the Lord himself* [no emissary, no archangel] *shall descend from heaven with a shout, with the voice of the archangel, and with the trump of God: and the dead in Christ* [bodies of the dead Christians] *shall rise first:*
17. *Then we which are alive and remain shall be caught up together with them in the clouds, to meet the Lord in the air: and so shall we ever be with the Lord.*
18. *Wherefore, comfort one another with these words."*

So, there are TWO KINDS of people who will be included in the Rapture:
1. "Dead in Christ" (Christians who have already died.)
2. Those Christians "which are alive and remain"

And if we understand that, then we can better understand what Jesus meant when He was talking to Martha, the sister of Lazarus, after Lazarus died:

John 11:25 - *"Jesus said unto her, I am the resurrection, and the life:* [the "resurrection" for those who are "dead in Christ"… and the "life" for those who are "alive and remain"] *he that believeth in me, though he were dead, yet shall he live:*

26   *And whosoever liveth and believeth in me shall never die…"*

NOW THAT'S THE RAPTURE OF THE CHURCH!

Now, let's talk about those new, glorified bodies that we're going to get IN THE RESURRECTION… AT THE RAPTURE.

What KIND of bodies will we receive?
What are those new glorified bodies going to be like?

The Apostle Paul goes into a lengthy discussion of the resurrected bodies of the saints in 1 Cor. 15. And he uses the analogy of seed being planted into the ground to speak of how our bodies will be very different when they are resurrected.

Just as a kernel of corn that is planted in the ground does not come up as a giant kernel of corn, but a corn plant, our bodies will also go into the ground one way and come up another way (very different).

1 Cor. 15:42 - *"So also is the resurrection of the dead* [reversal of physical death]. *It* [the body] *is sown* ["sown" like a seed in the ground… or buried] *in corruption, it is raised in incorruption:"*
"corruption" = in a mode of decay

43. *"It is sown in dishonor; it is raised in glory:*
That is, the body is buried in an "undignified state"… it has lost its color… it's lost its warmth…it is cold and lifeless… BUT it will be resurrected in its GLORIFIED state… full of life and warmth and beauty and vitality.

it is sown in weakness; it is raised in power:
In its weakness in its mortal state, the body is subject to illness, disease, and injury. It is WEAK in that even the most healthy, most developed, most muscular, most fit bodies are still prone to the ravages of disease. AND it is also weak in its abilities. Even the most accomplished athletes are still limited in what their bodies can do.

But, in our new GLORIFIED body, we will have power similar to that of Jesus. (Now, I'm not saying that we will EVER be exactly like Jesus and have all of His power. He is GOD. We are human…. And despite what some teach, we will NEVER be God or have the all the powers of God!)

However, you will remember that Jesus in His "glorified state" was not restrained by physical obstructions. When He met with His disciples after His resurrection, they were gathered in a room and it says that He suddenly just *appeared in their midst!*

Obviously, the Lord is not restrained by time, space, or physical obstructions. And even though I'm not sure about what degree we will have similar powers, you can be sure that our glorified state will be much more powerful than anything we possess in these mortal bodies!

44. *It is sown a natural body; it is raised a spiritual body. There is a natural body, and there is a spiritual body.*
So here it is…
The Scriptures say clearly that there is a "natural body"… That's the one that we living in now. And there is a "spiritual body"… or we could say a "glorified body" and that's the one that we are going to get in the resurrection.

45. *And so it is written, The first man Adam was made a living soul; the last Adam was made a quickening spirit.*
"the last Adam" = Jesus (the Scripture will say that in a couple of verses down)
Adam and Jesus are the two representative men of humanity. Through Adam came sin and from sin came death. Through Jesus came forgiveness of sin and from forgiveness comes life. Going back to:

1 Cor. 15:21-22 - *"For since by man, came death, by man came also the resurrection of the dead. For as in Adam all die, even so in Christ shall all be made alive."*

46.　*Howbeit that was not first which is spiritual, but that which is natural; and afterward that which is spiritual.*
There is always order to God's creation and plan. We are NOW living in the "natural body", but one day we will live in that new "spiritual body".

47.　*The first man is of the earth, earthy; the second man is the Lord from heaven.*
48.　*As is the earthy, such are they also that are earthy: and as is the heavenly, such are they also that are heavenly.*

In other words, those of us who are still in this mortal body, we are living in an earthy body just like Adam had. But when we receive that new glorified body, it will be like that heavenly body of our Lord Jesus.

49.　*And as we have borne the image of the earthy, we shall also bear the image of the heavenly.*
50.　*Now this I say, brethren, that flesh and blood cannot inherit the kingdom of God; neither doth corruption inherit incorruption.*

In other words, it would be impossible for us to enter into a perfect heaven in these imperfect bodies. Our present "natural bodies" are aging and deteriorating. They are corruptible. They would be completely unfit for the perfect, everlasting, environment of Heaven.

Now, look at verse 51…

51.　*Behold, I show you a mystery* [something that only God knows the answer to]; *We shall not all sleep* [there's that word again, meaning death… we shall not all die], *but we shall all* [all of us Christians who are alive and all those who have passed on] *be changed,*
Paul said that it is a mystery. Only God fully understands how He is going to give us that new, eternal, glorified body.

Now, look how fast it's going to happen…

52. *In a moment, in the twinkling of an eye, at the last trump:* [Notice that we will be changed into that new glorified body very quickly… in the twinkling of an eye, which some have calculated to be about 1/1000th of a second. And when will it happen? At the LAST trumpet sound. What is going to happen at the FIRST sound of the trumpet? The Dead IN Christ will be resurrected. So, we don't know how many sounds of the trumpet will be made at the Rapture, but there will be a first and a last.] *for the trumpet shall sound* [This is the first trumpet sound.], *and the dead shall be raised incorruptible, and we* [Those of us who are still alive at that time] *shall be changed.*

53. *For this corruptible must put on incorruption, and this mortal must put on immortality.*

54. *So when this corruptible shall have put on incorruption, and this mortal shall have put on immortality,* [In other words, when we've received our new glorified bodies] *then shall be brought to pass the saying that is written, Death is swallowed up in victory.*

55. *O death, where is thy sting? O grave, where is thy victory?* Now, *THAT's* the resurrection of the new, glorified bodies for all Christians who will have died by the time the Rapture takes place… AND the sudden changing (in the twinkling of an eye) of the body for those of us who are still living at the time of the Rapture… from this corruptible, mortal body to that beautiful, incorruptible, glorified body. And that change will be made for us on our way up!

This is the *promise* of God for every born again believer in Jesus Christ!

The Rapture
Quiz

1. There are _____ births, _____ deaths, and _____ resurrections.

2. Man is made up of three parts… _____, _____ and _____.

3. When a person dies the physical death, his _____ and _____ depart from his _____.

4. _____ is the reversal of physical death because the _____ and _____ re-enter the _____.

5. T or F   Only Christians are to be resurrected back to life.

6. The First Resurrection is the resurrection of the _____ and it will happen in three phases. We see it as the separate parts of the harvest:
    1. _____ _____ is the _____ _____ of the harvest.
    2. The _____ will be the _____ part of the harvest.
    3. The resurrection of the Tribulation saints will be the _____ of the harvest.

7. Paul told the Thessalonians in I Thess. 4:14, *"For if* [since] *we believe that Jesus died and rose again,* _____ _____ *them also which sleep in Jesus will God bring with him."* Which means that just as Jesus rose again, dead Christians will also rise again from the grave in the same way.

8. Who will meet Jesus in the air *first* at the Rapture?

9. T or F   The Bible teaches us that if we study the signs that point to the return of Jesus carefully, we can pinpoint the year (and possibly even the day) that He will come.

10. According to Matthew 24:33, the one thing that Jesus *does* expect His followers to *know* about His coming is when ____ ____ _____.

11. According to Rev. 6:15-17, the prevailing characteristic of the Tribulation from which we have been saved (according to I Thess. 1:10 and 5:9) is that it is a time of _____.

12. The doctrine of _____ is the belief that we should be looking for Jesus to return at any moment.

The Rapture
Quiz Answers

1. two, two, two

2. body, soul, and spirit

3. spirit and soul, body

4. Resurrection, spirit and soul, body

5. False (Dan. 12:2, John 5:28-29, Acts 24:15)

6. Redeemed
    1. Jesus Christ, first fruit
    2. Rapture, main
    3. Gleanings

7. even so

8. the "dead in Christ", or dead Christians

9. False. No one knows the day or the hour (Matt. 24:36)

10. it is near (the season)

11. wrath

12. Imminency

Lesson 2

The Jewish People

The Beginning of the Jewish people

Abraham's father, Terah, lived in "Ur" in the land of the Chaldees. Terah took his son, **Abram** (whose was name later changed to Abraham), Abram's wife, **Sarai** (whose name later changed to Sarah), and Abram's nephew, **Lot**, to move to the land of Canaan. However, they went as far as Haran and dwelt there until Terah died (Gen. 11:31-32).

Gen 11:31 - *"And Terah took Abram his son, and Lot the son of Haran his son's son, and Sarai his daughter in law, his son Abram's wife; and they went forth with them from Ur of the Chaldees, to go into the land of Canaan; and they came unto Haran, and dwelt there.*

32   And the days of Terah were two hundred and five years: and Terah died in Haran."

Then, God called Abram to leave Haran to "a land that I will show thee" (which was the land of Canaan) with the promise that He would make Abram into a great nation (Gen. 12:1-2).

Gen 12:1 - *"Now the Lord had said unto Abram, Get thee out of thy country, and from thy kindred, and from thy father's house, unto a land that I will shew thee:*

2   And I will make of thee a great nation, and I will bless thee, and make thy name great; and thou shalt be a blessing:"

Obviously, if God was going to make the descendants of Abram into a great nation, then that nation would have to have **land** to exist on. So, when they reached Canaan, God promised to give **"Abram's seed"** that land (Gen. 12:7).

Gen 12:7 - *"And the Lord appeared unto Abram, and said, **Unto thy seed will I give this land**: and there builded he an altar unto the Lord, who appeared unto him."*

Notice that the promise is in the future tense. In essence, God was saying that the day would come when He would give Abraham's descendants that land. Then, God later reaffirmed that covenant promise to Abram in Gen. 15:18. But by then, the giving of the land was already complete, so God speaks of it in a past tense, even though Abram at that time did not yet have any children.

Gen 15:18 - *"In the same day the Lord made a covenant with Abram saying,* **Unto thy seed have I given this land**, *from the river of Egypt unto the great river, the river Euphrates:"*

As a sign of God's promise with Abram and his descendants, God instituted the ritual of circumcision (Gen. 17:7-10). And, it was at this time that God changed Abram's name to Abraham ("father of a multitude") and Sarai's name to Sarah ("princess").

Gen 17:7 - *"And* **I will** *establish my covenant between me and thee and thy seed after thee in their generations for an* **everlasting covenant**, *to be a God unto thee, and to thy seed after thee.*

8   And I will give unto thee, and to thy seed after thee, the land wherein thou art a stranger, all the land of Canaan, for **an everlasting possession**; *and I will be their God.*

9   And God said unto Abraham, Thou shalt keep my covenant therefore, thou, and thy seed after thee in their generations.

10   This is my covenant, which ye shall keep, between me and you and thy seed after thee; Every man child among you shall be circumcised."

There's two aspects of God's covenant of **land ownership** with Abraham that we need to notice:

1. It was an **unconditional** covenant. God did not condition His giving of the land on the obedience of Abraham, or any other condition. He simply said, "I will" do this thing. It was a sovereign act of God!
2.   It was an **everlasting** covenant. That means it is STILL in effect today!

You probably remember the story of how God gave Abraham and Sarah a son in their old age… God had promised them a son (Gen. 15:4), but they were growing old and were still childless. So, Sarah offered her Egyptian hand maiden (Hagar) to Abraham to be a kind of surrogate mother to bear them a child. But when Hagar conceived Abraham's son (Ishmael), Sarah became jealous of her and gave her such a hard time that Hagar ran away. But an angel of the Lord found her and sent her back home with the promise that he would multiply the number of her offspring. So she gave birth to Ishmael when Abraham was 86 years old (Gen. 16:16).

Fourteen years later, when Abraham was 100 years old and Sarah was 90 years old, God fulfilled His promise and Isaac (the son of promise) was born to them. Isaac became the father of the Jewish people and Ishmael (and Esau) became the father of the Arabs.

However, God did not extend his land covenant that He made with Abraham to Ishmael, but specifically to Isaac. (Gen. 17:19-21).

Gen 17:19 - *"And God said, Sarah thy wife shall bear thee a son indeed; and thou shalt call his name* **Isaac: and I will establish my covenant with him for an everlasting covenant, and with his seed after him.**

20   *And as for Ishmael, I have heard thee: Behold, I have blessed him, and will make him fruitful, and will multiply him exceedingly; twelve princes shall he beget, and I will make him a great nation.*

21   **But my covenant will I establish with Isaac**, *which Sarah shall bear unto thee at this set time in the next year."*

Then, later when Isaac was a grown man, God reaffirmed that covenant directly to Isaac (Gen. 26:3).

Gen 26:2 - *"And the Lord appeared unto him* [Isaac], *and said, Go not down into Egypt; dwell in the land which I shall tell thee of:*

3   *Sojourn in this land, and I will be with thee, and will bless thee;* **for unto thee, and unto thy seed, I will give all these countries, and I will perform the oath which I sware unto Abraham thy father**;

4   *And I will make thy seed to multiply as the stars of heaven, and **will give unto thy seed all these countries**; and in thy seed shall all the nations of the earth be blessed;"*

Eventually, Isaac had twin sons, **Jacob and Esau** (Gen. 25:19-26), and God extended the Abrahamic Covenant (NOT to Esau but) to **Jacob** (Gen. 28:13). Jacob had a dream at Beth-El where he saw a ladder reaching up to Heaven with angels going up and down it.
Gen 28:13 - *"And, behold, the Lord stood above it, and said, I am the Lord God of Abraham thy father, and the God of Isaac: **the land whereon thou liest, to thee will I give it, and to thy seed**;"*

Then, later on, God appeared to Jacob again and changed his name to "Israel" and reaffirmed the land covenant promise to him (Gen. 35:11-12).

Gen 35:10 - *"And God said unto him, Thy name is Jacob: thy name shall not be called any more Jacob, but Israel shall be thy name: and he called his name Israel.*

11   *And God said unto him, I am God Almighty: be fruitful and multiply; a nation and a company of nations shall be of thee, and kings shall come out of thy loins;*

12   *And **the land which I gave Abraham and Isaac, to thee I will give it, and to thy seed after thee will I give the land**."*

Jacob had 12 sons who became the heads of the **Twelve Tribes of Israel** (Gen. 29:31–30:24, 35:16-18).

The Mosaic Covenant

God caused a famine to come upon the land of Canaan where Israel and his family lived. This, along with some God-orchestrated events in the life of Israel's 11th son (Joseph), were used by God to bring the twelve families of Israel down to the land of Egypt where they lived for some 400 years. During that time, they became a great nation. Eventually however, the pharaoh of Egypt began to see them as a national threat, so he began to force them into slavery hoping that it would reduce their numbers, but it didn't. So, he decreed that all the male children of the Hebrews were to be killed at birth, but once again, God foiled his plan by miraculously saving one particular baby named Moses, the one whom God would eventually use to lead the Israelites out of the Egyptian slavery.

At the appointed time, God used Moses through a series of plagues sent upon the Egyptians to free the children of Israel. And as Moses was leading them through the Sinai desert, God made another covenant with them. This covenant, unlike the Abrahamic covenant was **conditional**. God promised to bless them **IF** they were obedient to His commandments. But He also promised to curse them if they were disobedient, including removing them from the Promised Land that He had given them.

Exodus 19:5 - *Now therefore, **if** ye will obey my voice indeed, and keep my covenant, **then** ye shall be a peculiar treasure unto me above all people: for all the earth is mine:*

Deut. 28:1 - *And it shall come to pass, **if** thou shalt hearken diligently unto the voice of the LORD thy God, to observe and to do all his commandments which I command thee this day, that the LORD thy God will set thee on high above all nations of the earth:*

*2.   And all these blessings shall come on thee, and overtake thee, **if** thou shalt hearken unto the voice of the LORD thy God.*

In the next **12 verses** (Deut. 28:3-14), God lists the many blessing He will give the Israelites if they would obey His commandments (great productivity in having children, raising livestock, and growing crops; strength to defeat their enemies, etc.). **But** in the next **54 verses** (Deut. 28:15-68), He describes all the curses that He will place upon them if they are NOT obedient, including taking them out of the land He had given them (Deut. 28:63).

Basically, God's requirement for Israel was **Holiness** (Lev. 20:7-8) because they were to His representatives to the rest of the world.

Leviticus 20:7 - *Sanctify yourselves therefore, and be ye holy: for I am the LORD your God.*

8. *And ye shall keep my statutes, and do them: I am the LORD which sanctify you.*

Exodus 19:6 - *And ye shall be unto me a kingdom of priests, and an holy nation.*

This covenant with the people of Israel had nothing to do with the **ownership** of the land (that was a settled issue in God's unconditional, everlasting covenant that He had made with Abraham), but dealt with **possession** of the land. It is possible to OWN something and yet not POSSESS it. And God made it clear that if they became disobedient to His commandments, He would dispossess them from the land He had given them (even though they would never lose ownership of it).

We know from the Biblical story that the Israelites did NOT continue to obey God's commandments. Those early generations were faithful and obedient, but just as it happens in an individual's life, they gradually began to depart from God's instructions and subsequent generations became ever further removed from the strict obedience that God required of them.

So, in adherence to His own covenant Word that He gave through Moses, God used other nations to defeat Israel and take them from their land. And this actually happened TWO TIMES!

First, the Babylonians defeated Judah in 586 BC and carried them away into captivity for seventy years, after which, they were allowed by the Persians to return and rebuild their Temple and the city walls (see Ezra and Nehemiah).

Daniel was one of the Israelites who was carried away captive into Babylon. And through his understanding of God's Word, he knew WHY this captivity had happened. In a beautiful prayer to God, Daniel confessed the sin of his people.

Dan. 9:11 - *Yea, **all Israel have transgressed thy law**, even by departing, that they might not obey thy voice; therefore **the curse is poured upon us, and the oath that <u>written in the law of Moses</u>** the servant of God, because we have sinned against him.*

As Daniel said, the people had broken "the law of Moses", which of course, was the Mosaic Covenant that God had made with them through Moses.

Then, a little over six hundred years later, when Israel was under the rule of the Romans, they made the same mistake again. About forty years before this second scattering of the Jews, Jesus prophesied that it would happen. One day shortly before His crucifixion, as Jesus and his disciples walked out of the beautiful second Temple in Jerusalem, He said,

Matt. 24:2 - *And Jesus said unto them, See ye not all these things?* [speaking of the Temple complex in Jerusalem] *verily I say unto you, There shall not be left here one stone upon another, that shall not be thrown down.*

About forty years later, in 70 AD, in response to a rebellion started by the Jews in Capernaum, the Romans besieged Jerusalem for 143 days (according to Josephus). When they succeeded in breaking through the city walls, they completely destroyed Jerusalem and the Temple. It was a horrible blood bath as the Roman soldiers showed no mercy upon the citizens, killing all but 95,000 of its inhabitants which they exported as slaves to the four corners of the Roman Empire. So complete was the destruction of the Temple that literally every stone in its construction was thrown down. Just as Jesus had prophesied, not one stone was left upon another.

This second destruction of the Temple in Jerusalem and the scattering of the Jews is known as the **Grand Diaspora** (the Great Dispersion). For over eighteen centuries, the scattered Jews were a people without a land. Even though they by divine right still OWNED the land of Israel, they were removed from it for centuries. They were "the wandering Jew". This came in fulfillment of many prophecies, including the promise that God had given them through Moses of what He would do if they became disobedient.

Deut. 28:63 - *And it shall come to pass, that as the LORD rejoiced over you to do you good, and to multiply you; so the LORD will rejoice over you to destroy you, and to bring you to nought; and ye shall be plucked from off the land whither thou goest to possess it.*

64.   *And the LORD shall scatter thee among all people, from the one end of the earth even unto the other; and there thou shalt serve other gods, which neither thou nor thy fathers have known, even wood and stone.*

65.   *And among these nations shalt thou find no ease, neither shall the sole of thy foot have rest: but the LORD shall give thee there a trembling heart, and failing of eyes, and sorrow of mind:*

This great dispersion of the Jewish people surpassed any horror that they had ever experienced or had imagined.

When the Jewish leaders brought Jesus before Pilate, demanding that He be crucified, he was reluctant to execute Jesus and eventually,

Matthew 27:24 - *When Pilate saw that he could prevail nothing, but that rather a tumult was made, he took water, and washed his hands before the multitude, saying, I am innocent of the blood of this just person; see ye to it.*

25   *Then answered all the people, and said,* **His blood be on us, and on our children.**

This acceptance by the Jews of the murder of Jesus, along with the general apostate condition of all the Jews, brought untold suffering upon themselves. Just about 40 years later, they were destroyed by the Romans and for over eighteen centuries, they were scattered. And during that time, for the most part, they were viciously persecuted.

Look at this brief overview of their suffering:

1.   70 AD - The Roman general Titus destroyed Jerusalem and the Temple, killing one million Jews and taking 97,000 captive as slaves. NOTE - The prophet Daniel had prophesied that the city and the sanctuary (Temple) would be destroyed by the people of the Antichrist (Danl. 9:26). This gives us evidence as to the origin of the coming "Man of Sin", the Antichrist.

2.   135 AD - Hadrian came back to the land of Palestine to make a final a final and complete destruction of the rebellious Jews. He killed some 580,000 Jews, fulfilling

   Micah 3:12 - *Therefore shall Zion for your sake be plowed as a field, and Jerusalem shall become heaps, and the mountain of the house as the high places of the forest.*

   (Some would say that Micah's prophecy was fulfilled by the destruction by the Babylonians in 586 BC, but a more complete fulfillment seems to have been made by the Romans in their campaign to decimate the Jews one final time and thus remove all chances of a future Jewish rebellion against their empire. Hadrian came with a vengeance and Israel was *"plowed as a field".*)

3. 1020 AD - All Jews were banished from England and in 1096 AD, the "Holy War" (Crusades) started in which thousands of Jews were murdered in Europe.

4. 1306 AD - In France, 100,000 Jews were stripped of their possessions and run out of the country.

5. 1348 AD - The plague of the "Black Death" pandemic swept through Europe killing a fourth of the population and the Jews were blamed for it. Therefore, they were tortured, boiled, and burned to death by the thousands.

6. 1400-1600 AD - In the Spanish Inquisition, untold thousands of Jews were tortured to death with indescribable brutality.

7. 1941-1945 AD - In the Holocaust, some six million Jews were slaughtered by the Nazis. Even a summary reading of the history of the Holocaust will give the reader a sickened feeling of disgust and dread in the way that the Jews were mistreated by the *and failing of eyes, and sorrow of mind"* (Deut. 28:65).

The Return of the Jewish People

And yet, even before this second dispersion and suffering ever began, God's prophetic Word said the day would come when He would gather them back into their homeland, never to be uprooted again.

Isaiah 11:11 - *And it shall come to pass in that day, that the Lord shall set his hand again **the second time** to recover the remnant of his people, which shall be left, from Assyria, and from Egypt, and from Pathros, and from Cush, and from Elam, and from Shinar, and from Hamath, and from **the islands of the sea**.*

12. *And he shall set up an ensign for the nations, and shall assemble the outcasts of Israel, and gather together the dispersed of Judah **from the four corners of the earth**.*

Notice that verse 12 says that God will bring together *"the outcasts of Israel"* (the ten tribes of the northern kingdom) and *"the dispersed of*

Judah" (the two tribes of the southern kingdom). In other words, this final regathering will be the Jewish people OF ALL TWELVE TRIBES.

Ezekiel 36:24 - *For I will take you from among the heathen, and gather you **out of all countries**, and will bring you into **your own land**.*

Ezekiel 37:21 - *And say unto them, Thus saith the Lord GOD; Behold, I will take the children of Israel from among the heathen, whither they be gone, and will gather them on every side, and bring them **into their own land**:*

22a *And I will make them **one nation** in the land upon the mountains of Israel...*

So, how has God accomplished the monumental task of bringing a worldwide dispersion of people back to their ancient homeland... a land that had been abused into a wasteland for centuries... a land that was occupied by Arab bandits? How would He motivate them to go HOME?

The Zionist Movement (the movement to establish a homeland for the Jews and to bring them there) began in the late 1800's with the first Zionist Congress held in Basel, Switzerland in 1897. Theodor Herzl (considered to be the founder of the Zionist movement and the "father" of modern day Israel) resided as president. When Mr. Herzl (who was not a religious man) stood to the podium, he said that it was his belief that the nation of Israel would be born within 50 years. How prophetic were his words! Fifty years later, in 1947, the United Nations partitioned the land of Israel (then called Palestine) giving a portion of it to the Jews, which led to their declaration of independence a year later on May 14, 1948.

On Nov. 2, 1917, during WWI, the Balfour Declaration was written in Great Britain expressing their desire to establish a Jewish homeland in the land of Palestine.

During WWI, Turkey (the Ottoman Empire) joined with Germany and the Central Powers of Europe to fights against the Allies. So, after they were defeated, the land of Palestine was taken from them by the League of Nations (the forerunner of the United Nations) and given to Great Britain as a mandate (an overseer) and Jewish immigration continued under Great Britain's oversight for the next 30 years.

In 1948, Great Britain pulled out of Palestine. On the day they left, Israel declared her independence... **May 14, 1948**. To this day, Jews continue to immigrate to Israel and today, there are over six million Jews in Israel.

And not only did God say that He would bring them back to their land, but He also said that once He did this, they would NEVER be plucked up out of their land again.

Amos 9:15 - *And I will plant them upon their land, and **they shall no more be pulled up out of their land** which I have given them, saith the LORD thy God.*

(See also Jer. 24:6)

This gathering of the Jewish people back into their homeland will be consummated during the coming period of time that we call The Tribulation, which will be used to ultimately bring a remnant of them into a saving relationship with their true Messiah, Jesus Christ.

The Time of Jacob's (Israel's) Trouble

Near the end of the seventy year captivity of the Jewish people in which Daniel was in Babylon, God revealed to him that He had determined that there would be another 70 weeks of years required to *"finish the transgression"* of the Jews (Daniel's people) and *"bring in everlasting righteousness"*.

Daniel 9:24 - *Seventy weeks* [actually, 70 "periods of seven" which in this context is obviously a reference to periods of 7 years] *are determined upon* **thy people** *and upon thy holy city,* **to finish the transgression,** *and to make an end of sins, and to make reconciliation for iniquity, and* **to bring in everlasting righteousness,** *and to seal up the vision and prophecy, and to anoint the most Holy.*

In the next three verses, God divides this 490 years into three periods of

        7 weeks - 7 x 7 =   49 yrs.
        62 weeks - 62 x 7 = 434 yrs.
        1 week – 1 x 7 =   **7 yrs.**
                          ----
                          490 yrs.

Verse 26 says that after the 62 week period *"shall Messiah be cut off"* (He will be killed). We won't take time here to show how this calculation works (we'll look at it later), but on that exact year, Jesus was crucified in Jerusalem!

Then, it was as if God stopped his clock on the fulfillment of the 490 years and turned His attention to the Gentile nations of the world to gather a special group together called The Church. When the Church (the "Bride" of Christ) is complete, then the "Groom" (Jesus) will come for His Bride (the Rapture) and this Age of Grace (the Church Age) will be finished.

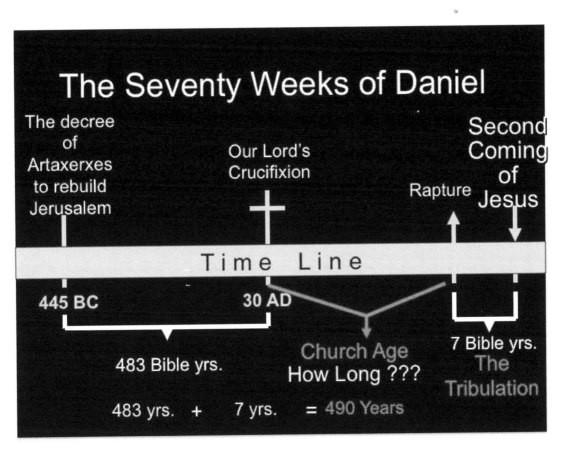

The Seventy Weeks of Daniel

But this leaves one more period of seven years that God said He would deal with Daniel's people, so He will turn His attention back to that task in the seven year period following the Rapture that we call The Tribulation. God will use this horrific time in history to bring a remnant of the Jews into an everlasting relationship with Jesus Christ. It will end with the appearance of Jesus coming in great power and glory to usher in "everlasting righteousness" (Matt. 24:30).

There are different names used for this last seven years before our Lord's return to earth. Some refer to it "Daniel's Seventieth Week" (Dan. 9:24-27). Jeremiah called it the "Time of Jacob's Trouble (Jer. 30:7) and the Apostle Paul said it is the time of "the Wrath To Come" (1 Thess. 1:10). But Jesus called it the time of "Tribulation" (Matt. 24:21).

It is during this seven year period of time (especially the last half of it) when God will use unprecedented persecution of the Jews to bring them to their knees (Dan. 9:27, Jer. 30:4-7, 15, Zech. 13:8, Rev. 6, 8-9, 12:17). And just at the last moment when it looks like they will be utterly annihilated, Jesus (their true Messiah) will appear in the sky to destroy their enemies and rescue the remnant that is still alive. This group will turn to Jesus as their true Messiah and Savior en masse (Jer. 30:8-11, Zech. 12:10, 13:1,9, Isa. 12, 66:8, Zeph. 3:13-20, Rom. 11:26-27).

Romans 11:26 – *And so all Israel shall be saved: as it is written, There shall come out of Zion The Deliverer, and shall turn away ungodliness from Jacob:*
27 *For this is my covenant unto them, when I shall take away their sins.*

The Lord will then establish His Millennial Kingdom here on planet earth in which He will rule in peace, justice, and righteousness for 1000 years. His throne will be in Jerusalem and all the land that God promised to the descendants of Abraham (Gen. 15:18) will be the home of those Jews He saved. Among the nations of the world, Israel will become the head of all nations (Zech. 2:10-12, 8:7-8, 8:23, Isa. 45:14-17, 60:1-16).

Isaiah 60:1 - *Arise, shine; for thy light is come, and the glory of the Lord is risen upon thee...*

3 *And the Gentiles shall come to thy light, and kings to the brightness of thy rising...*

12 *For the nation and kingdom that will not serve thee shall perish; yea, those nations shall be utterly wasted.*

The Jewish People
Quiz

1. God called Abram out of the city of _____ *"unto a land that I will show thee".*

2. In the covenant that God made with Abram, He said that He would make of Abram a great _____.

3. God instituted the ritual of _____ as a sign of the covenant that he had made with Abram.

4. According to the Abrahamic Covenant in Gen. 12:7, God gave to Abram's descendants the _____ in Canaan and it extended from the river of _____ to the river _____ in modern day Iraq (Gen. 15:18).

5. Two significant feature of the Abrahamic Covenant that God made was that it was _____ and _____.

6. God extended the covenant that He made with Abraham to his son _____ and to his son _____ and his descendants.

7. The twelve sons of _____, whom God renamed _____, became the heads of the twelve tribes of Israel.

8. God made a covenant with Israel through Moses in which He said He would bless them if they obeyed Him and that He would curse them if they did not obey Him. We call this a _____ covenant. Of the curses that God promised them for their disobedience, one was that He would _____ _____ _____ _____ _____.

9. The Abrahamic Covenant dealt with the _____ of the land and it was unconditional. Whereas the Mosaic Covenant dealt with the _____ of the land based on the condition that they obeyed Him.

10. The Jews were removed from their land twice. The first time was in 586 BC by the _____. The second time was in 70 AD by the _____.

11. Isaiah 11:10 says, *"And it shall come to pass in that day, that the Lord shall set His hand again the* _____ _____ *to recover the remnant of His people, which shall be left..."*

12. And God promises in Amos 9:15, *"And I will plant them upon their land, and they shall __ ____ __ _____ __ ___ __ _____ ____ which I have given them, saith the Lord thy God."*

13. The Jewish people began to migrate back to Palestine in the late 1800's in what was called the _____ Movement.

14. Israel declared herself an independent and sovereign nation on _____ (date).

15. The Jewish people will suffer great persecution in the time of the Tribulation. That's why Jeremiah calls it "The Time of _____ _____" (Jer. 30:7).

The Jewish People
Quiz Answers

1. Haran (Gen. 12:4)

2. nation (Gen. 12:2)

3. circumcision (Gen. 17:10)

4. land, Egypt, Euphrates (Gen. 15:18)

5. everlasting, unconditional (Gen. 17:8)

6. Isaac, Jacob (Gen. 17:19-21, 28:13-15)

7. Jacob, Israel

8. conditional, remove them from their land (Deut. 28:63)

9. ownership, possession

10. Babylonians, Romans

11. second time

12. no more be pulled up out of their land

13. Zionist

14. May 14, 1948

15. Jacob's Trouble

Lesson 3

<u>The Time of the Gentiles</u>

In the second year of King Nebuchadnezzar's reign (this would have been two years after his father died, around 603 BC), he had a terrible dream. And even though he could not remember exactly what the dream was, it plagued his consciousness with such dread that he couldn't even sleep because of it.

Daniel 2:1 - *And in the second year of the reign of Nebuchadnezzar, Nebuchadnezzar dreamed dreams, wherewith his spirit was troubled, and his sleep brake from him.*

Unlike any other empire that ever existed, the Babylonian Empire under King Nebuchadnezzar was a true autocracy. He had absolute power in all the affairs of his kingdom. His word was law and unquestioned. There was no command from him that would be thought too strange, unreasonable, illogical, or irrational for his subjects. Without questioning his reasons, every command of Nebuchadnezzar was immediately carried out. Among men, he was all-powerful.

But now, he was confronted with this dream that had him haggled and completely undone. ***"Why is this DREAM eating at me?"***, he must've thought. "Surely the gods are trying to reveal some great message to me that I cannot decipher! I ***must*** have an answer to this strange occurrence before it drives me insane!"

So, like any man of means would do, he called in the "experts" in the field of dreams and interpretations. He brought in the *"magicians, and the astrologers, and the sorcerers, and Chaldeans"* of his great kingdom (the wise men) and demanded that they
    (1)   Tell him what his dream was and
    (2)   Tell him what the interpretation of it was.

He threatened them that if they were unable to reveal to him his dream and its interpretation, that they would be *"cut in pieces, and your houses shall be made a dunghill."* (Dan. 2:5) And old Neb was a man that could do exactly that! But even this man of such power was unable to find relief from this constant burden of his mind because his wise men were clueless as to how to answer their king.

Well, despite their arguments that the king was asking an impossibility, King Nebuchadnezzar's mind was not changed and he ordered all the wise men of Babylon put to death.

Daniel 2:13 - *And the decree went forth that the wise men should be slain; and they sought Daniel and his fellows to be slain.*

It appears that Daniel and his three Hebrew buddies (Hananiah, Mishael, and Azariah), even though they were considered to be a part of that group of "wise men of Babylon", were not present when this initial conversation took place between the wise men and the king. No doubt, God did this to show the complete incompetence of these other so-called "wise men".

So when the soldiers came to get Daniel for execution, he was told by the captain of the guard about the king's decree. Daniel immediately requested to speak to the king and was granted his audience. (This in itself was miracle because it was nearly impossible to get to speak directly to the king.) So, Daniel went in to speak to King Nebuchadnezzar and requested from him that he be given time to answer the king's questions. And, it appears that King Nebuchadnezzar gave Daniel a 24 hour reprieve from the execution order... time to come up with the answers about the dream.

Daniel then went to his three friends and asked them to join him in beseeching *"the God of heaven concerning this secret"* (Dan. 2:18). That night, God answered their prayers and revealed the dream and its interpretation to Daniel in a vision.

The next day, Daniel went in to the king's presence and told him that there is a God in heaven that *"revealeth secrets, and maketh known to the king Nebuchadnezzar **what shall be in the latter days**."*.

Daniel 2:27 - *Daniel answered in the presence of the king, and said, The secret which the king hath demanded cannot the wise men, the astrologers, the magicians, the soothsayers, show unto the king;*

28   *But there is a God in heaven that revealeth secrets, and maketh known to the king Nebuchadnezzar **what shall be in the latter days**. Thy dream, and the vision of thy head upon thy bed, are these;*

Once again, we see the humility of Daniel in that he did not present himself as the revealer of secrets, but simply as one whom God was using to bear the message to the king. The theme of this dream and its interpretation is set forth from the outset. It was a message about the things that would happen **in the latter days**.

The term "latter days" is used nine times in the Bible, all of them in the Old Testament. It is always a reference to the last days of the age leading up to the coming of the Messiah Who will then establish His kingdom of everlasting righteousness. So, God's revelation to Nebuchadnezzar was to be an explanation of those latter days of the age that will usher in the Messiah and His Kingdom.

Daniel explained to King Nebuchadnezzar what his dream was. It went like this:

He said that the king had dreamed of a great statue (an *"image"* of a man) that had an extremely frightening appearance.

Its head was made of gold…
Its chest and arms were made of silver…
Its stomach was made of brass…
Its legs were made of iron…
And its feet were made of a non-homogeneous mixture of iron and clay.

Suddenly, a stone that was not carved by man, came flying through the air and hit the statue on its feet of iron and clay, causing the entire statue to fall and shattering all the elements of its make-up (the gold, silver, brass, iron, and iron/clay) into tiny pieces, which the wind then blew away like so much chaff in the wind (*"no place was found for them"*, Dan. 2:35). Then, the stone that hit the statue began to grow and grow until it became a great mountain that dominated the entire earth.

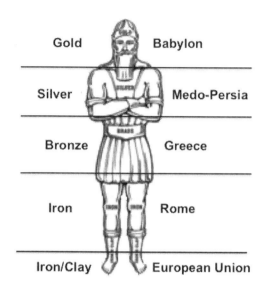

Beginning in verse 36, Daniel interprets the meaning of the king's dream. He said:

(1) The gold head of the statue was representative of King Nebuchadnezzar and his great Babylonian empire.

(2) After the Babylonian empire would come another empire, inferior to his, represented by the chest and arms of silver.

(3) This "silver empire" would be followed by a third empire symbolically represented by the stomach of brass.

(4) This "brass empire" would eventually be replaced by a great and strong empire symbolized by the strength of the iron legs.

Then, he says:

Daniel 2:41 - *And whereas thou sawest the feet and toes, part of potters' clay and part of iron,* **the kingdom** [referring to the "iron kingdom" of the legs] *shall be divided; but there shall be in it of the strength of the iron, forasmuch as thou sawest the iron mixed with miry clay.*

You will notice that the feet of iron and clay are not spoken of as another empire or, as the fifth empire. But rather, they are referred to as a continuation of *"the kingdom"* (the "iron empire" in vs. 41) in the time when it will be *"divided"*. Even though there is a lack of unity in this period of the iron empire, it still possesses **some** strength (the iron), but it is plagued with a kind of weakness (the clay) as well.

Verse 42 says *"so the kingdom shall be partly strong, and partly* **broken**.*"* The word translated as "broken" is the Hebrew word "tebar", meaning "to be divided or fragmented".

Daniel goes on to say that in the days of these kings (of the iron/clay empire), that the God of heaven will destroy all of man's kingdoms and establish His own everlasting kingdom. And His kingdom will *"stand forever"*.

Daniel 2:44 - *And in the days of these kings shall the God of heaven set up a kingdom, which shall never be destroyed: and the kingdom shall not be left to other people, but it shall break in pieces and consume all these kingdoms, and* **it shall stand for ever**.

From the time of the first kingdom of gold (the Babylonian empire) until the destruction of the last part of the iron kingdom which will be the iron/clay period, we have represented in Nebuchadnezzar's dream statue the **"Time of the Gentiles"**.

It is a time period with a specific beginning and a definite end... a time that exalts man as god in opposition to the true God of the universe, Jesus Christ.

Now, in Daniel 3, we read the story of how Nebuchadnezzar built a golden statue of himself (a statue of *a man*) in the plain of Dura that was **60 cubits** high and **six cubits** wide. Then, he put together a **six-man** band and commanded the people to fall down and worship the statue when they heard the music begin to play. Notice the use of the number 6.

Throughout the Bible, **the number six is the number of man**. Man was created on the sixth day of creation week and commanded to labor for six days. Six is one less than seven, which is the number for completion or perfection. Man, in all of his attempts at righteousness can never be perfectly righteous. *"For all have sinned and come short of the glory of God."* (Rom. 3:23)

So, from the time of Nebuchadnezzar's attempt to deify himself through his "statue of six" to the last Gentile leader of the world whose name will be numerically represented by the number 666, who will also have a statue of himself that he commands people to worship (Rev. 13:14-15), we see that **"the Time of the Gentiles" is a time when man desires to be worshipped and attempts to be god**. From Nebuchadnezzar and his "gold empire" to the last days "iron/clay empire", the "Time of the Gentiles" is the time of man. So, Nebuchadnezzar's dream is of **a metallic statue of a man**.

Jesus declared in the book of Luke,

Luke 21:24 - *And they* [the Jews] *shall fall by the edge of the sword, and shall be led away captive into all nations; and **Jerusalem shall be trodden down of the Gentiles, until the times of the Gentiles be fulfilled***.

In other words, Jerusalem will only come from under the control of the Gentiles when the time of the Gentiles comes to an end... that is, when Jesus, the Messiah returns to destroy that last Gentile kingdom, the "iron/clay" kingdom. Jesus, The Rock, will annihilate the last vestige of man's attempt to be god and will establish His own everlasting kingdom. Thus will "the time of the Gentiles" come to an end.

Identification of the Gentile Empires

So, what are the four Gentile empires pictured in the statue of Nebuchadnezzar's dream? The first one is clearly identified by Daniel in his interpretation of the dream. He said to Nebuchadnezzar, *"Thou art this head of gold."* (Dan. 2:38). So, the Babylonian Empire is the first empire. But God did not, at this time, reveal to Daniel the identity of the other three empires.

However, later on in chapter eight, in the vision of the Ram and He-goat, God reveals to Daniel what Empires no. 2 and 3 would be. Empire no. 2 would be the **Medo-Persian Empire** and it would be followed by empire no. 3, the **Greek Empire**:
Daniel 8:20-21a - *The ram which thou sawest having two horns are **the kings of Media and Persia**. And the rough goat **is the king of Grecia**...*
(We'll talk more about this vision of the Ram and the He-goat later).

Well, the Babylonians were defeated by the Medo-Persian empire in 539 BC. And Daniel gives us the account of the fall of the last Babylonian king, Belshazzar, in chapter five in the story of the hand of God writing on the wall *"Thou art weighed in the balances and found wanting"*. So, Daniel lived long enough to see the fall of the Babylonian Empire and the rise of Empire No. 2 (the Medo-Persian empire). This joint empire of the Medes and Persians is represented by the two arms (and chest) of silver in Nebuchadnezzar's dream statue.

The Persians (who were the stronger side of this joint empire) were defeated when a very accomplished, military genius named Alexander the Great, led the Greeks from the west to defeat them at Gaugamela.

Then, in Daniel 9, God reveals to Daniel that the Temple in Jerusalem would be rebuilt (you'll remember that Daniel was in the Babylonian captivity after Neb. had destroyed Jerusalem and the Temple) and that this second Temple would also be destroyed by *"the people of the prince that shall come"* Dan. 9:26), a reference to the coming Antichrist. Well, we know from history who did that… It was the Romans who eventually overthrew the Greek empire and it was the Romans who also eventually destroyed Jerusalem and the Temple in 70 AD.

So, when this is all put together, we have the identity of the four great gentile empires that would rule over the land of Palestine:

(1)   Babylonian Empire
(2)   Medo-Persian Empire
(3)   Greek Empire
(4)   Roman Empire

Daniel 7 – More Information About the Fourth Empire

Now, let's look at Daniel 7 for a moment…
Because in chapter seven (the first year of Belshazzar's reign, the last king of the Babylonian Empire to rule over the city of Babylon), God confirmed to Daniel the succession of these four gentile empires in another dream about four strange beasts that come up out of the sea.

(1)   The first beast that comes up is a lion with eagle's wings (the winged lion was actually the national symbol of the Babylonian Empire).

(2)   The second beast was a bear that *"raised up itself on one side"* showing that one side was stronger than the other side. And it says in Dan. 7:5 that it was told to *"Arise, devour much flesh"*. This is descriptive of how the Persians defeated their enemies by overwhelming them huge numbers of soldiers. They were very slow to move, but very powerful, like a big bear.

(3)   The third beast was a leopard with four wings. As a leopard is a very swift animal, and with the addition of the four wings, it symbolized that it was an empire that moved very fast. The Greek Empire, led by Alexander the Great conquered many kingdoms… all the way to India, in just ten years. Such speedy conquest of such a vast area was unprecedented.

(4)   The last of the four beasts was *"dreadful and terrible, and strong exceedingly; and it had great **iron** teeth"* (Dan. 7:7)… a kind of non-descript monster beast. This is descriptive of the Roman

Empire that destroyed everything in its path with great cruelty and brutality.

No doubt, Daniel immediately understood that these four beasts were symbolic of the four great gentile empires revealed in Nebuchadnezzar's dream some *fifty years* before and that the **iron-toothed** beast (number four) was symbolic of the same empire as the iron legs in the statue of Nebuchadnezzar's dream. (Sometimes, we get impatient in waiting on our answers from God. Daniel, who undoubtedly had many questions about Nebuchadnezzar's dream, waited *fifty years* before God began to reveal some of the details about the nations of "the Times of the Gentiles".)

But then, God gives Daniel some additional information about that fourth kingdom. Daniel saw something very strange about that fourth beast. He saw that it had ten horns on its head. And as he was looking at it, suddenly another "little horn" began to grow out among the ten horns, **uprooting three of the ten horns as it grew up**.

Daniel 7:15-16 says that Daniel was perplexed and troubled after seeing this vision, so he questioned the interpreter of this dream (presumably an angel standing near him) what the truth of all this was about. Again, if he didn't know it before, the angel explained first of all that the four beasts were four kings (kingdoms).

But strangely enough, Daniel did not ask for the identity of beast numbers two and three. (He already knew that the first one was the Babylonian empire.) He apparently was so impressed with the awesome power of the fourth beast, that he skipped right over asking about the second and third beasts and asked about the *fourth beast.*

Dan. 7:19 - ***Then I would know the truth of the fourth beast***, *which was diverse from all the others, exceeding dreadful, whose teeth were of iron, and his nails of brass; which devoured, brake in pieces and stamped the residue with his feet;*

Whereupon, the angel began to reveal much information about the fourth great gentile kingdom that would exist just prior to the Lord's coming to establish His own everlasting kingdom.

In the vision, Daniel saw that the "little horn" that grew up among the ten, was different from the ten horns because it had *"eyes like the eyes of a man, and a mouth speaking great things"* (Dan. 7:8).

Now, in Bible prophecy, a "horn" is symbolic of a king or some other person of power and authority. And, in fact, this is the interpretation that is given to Daniel about the ten horns later on in Daniel 7:24 where it says *"And the ten horns out of this kingdom **are ten kings** that shall arise"*. This is also symbolized in Nebuchadnezzar's dream by the ten toes on the statue.

And then, it goes on to say about the little horn that came up... *"and another shall arise after them; and he shall be diverse* [different] *from the first, and he shall subdue three kings"*. This "little horn" that comes up by uprooting three of the ten horns is none other than that coming world leader, the Antichrist, who will come to power by overthrowing three of the ten kings.

Now, in Rev. 17, we find that **all ten of these last days kings** are still in power when the Lord comes. So, what will probably happen is that the Antichrist will come to power by subduing three of the ten kings. And then, he will replace them with three more kings and make himself the supreme leader of all ten.

Look at it. In Revelation 17, this final empire is represented again as a beast with ten horns, the same as the ten horns on Daniel's beast. There, it says they (the ten kings) will *"give their power and strength unto the beast"* [the Antichrist].

Rev. 17:12 - *And the ten horns which thou sawest are ten kings, which have received no kingdom as yet; but receive power as kings one hour with the beast.*
13 *These have one mind, and **shall give their power and strength unto the beast.***
14 ***These shall make war with the Lamb*** [Jesus], *and the Lamb shall overcome them; for he is Lord of lords, and King of kings; and they that are with him are called and chosen, and faithful.*

So, the ten kings of this final empire will still be in power when Jesus comes and He will destroy them. Obviously though, they will be subordinates of the "beast" (Antichrist) to whom they will *give their power and strength".*

So, that last days period (the Iron/Clay period) of the Roman Empire is to be ruled initially by ten "kings". In today's terminology, it will more likely be some kind of ten-man ruling board (committee). These ten leaders are also represented by John in Rev. 13 as ten horns on a single beast that is a composite of the four beasts of Daniel 7.

Now, there are many thoughts on what the meaning is in Daniel 7:41-43 where it says that they will be partly strong like iron and partly weak like clay. Let me suggest a couple of interpretations that seem to fit best.

1.   One is the idea that these ten leaders will be demonically possessed, which be their strength, but because of they are still human beings, they will also have the weakness of human mortals. 2:43 says, *"And whereas thou sawest iron mixed with miry clay,* **they shall mingle themselves with the seed of men***; but they shall not cleave one to another, even as iron is not mixed with clay."*

Rev. 17:16-17 also tells us that these leaders will become jealous of the wealth of the world religious system and will overthrow it and say that all honor and glory should be given to the Antichrist as the supreme god and ruler of this world. It could be because their demon possession that they make such a proclamation.

2.   The other idea has more to do with the political systems that have developed over the course of centuries known as the Time of the Gentiles. The first empire (Babylonian led by Nebuchadnezzar) was an absolute autocracy, which means that one man had total control. It's not a very equitable system, but it is very strong. There are no "checks and balances" in the system, so when that one man makes a decree, it is done without question. Again, this doesn't usually lead to freedom and prosperity for the individual citizens in the kingdom, but it is very powerful and effective in getting things done.

From that, government has developed into a democratic system that gives every citizen some control over policy making (through their voting rights). Democracy, even though it is very beneficial to the individual citizens, it is "weak" in that it is very difficult to get things done (laws passed).

So, the strength of the iron (the old Roman system of being led by the Caesars) will be weakened through the democratic process that will no doubt elect the ten kings.

But one thing is for sure... Because these men are represented at the very end of the statue (the toes), this will be the FINAL power base over the Revived Roman Empire (until Antichrist takes control of all of it) and then the Lord returns to destroy it.

Now, as I said, even though the angel does not specifically **give the name** of the fourth empire to Daniel, we can easily identify from world history that the fourth great gentile kingdom is none other than **THE ROMAN EMPIRE** that ruled the civilized world for some five hundred years.

Now, lets look briefly at the vision of the Ram and the He-Goat in chapter eight...

Daniel 8 - Another Little Horn

Two years later, in the eighth chapter of Daniel, God gives His prophet yet another vision that **fills in the gap** about the identity of the second and third empires (the silver and brass on Nebuchadnezzar's dream statue, and the second and third beasts in Daniel's vision in chapter seven). In this vision, Daniel sees a ram standing next to the river Ulai that has two horns, one larger than the other. Suddenly, a he-goat with one large horn between his eyes came charging from the west and destroyed the ram. Then, the large horn on the he-goat was broken off and four other horns came up in its place. And then, out of one of those four horns came another "little horn" that *"waxed exceeding great, toward the south, and toward the east, and toward the pleasant land* [the land of Palestine]*."* (Dan. 8:9).

As we've already said, the angel Gabriel gave Daniel the interpretation of his vision in which the ram with two horns is identified as the kings of **Media and Persia** and the he-goat with the one big horn that destroyed the ram was the kingdom of **Greece,** headed by its first great king which we know was Alexander the Great.

Daniel 8:20 - *The ram which thou sawest having two horns are **the kings of Media and Persia***.
21   *And the rough goat **is the king of Grecia** ; and the great horn that is between his eyes is the first king.*

But then, in the vision, Daniel said that the one big horn on that he-goat (Alexander the Great) was broken off. And in its place, grew up *"four notable ones toward the four winds of heaven"* (Dan. 8:8). And out of one of those four horns, a "little horn" grew out.

As I said, the one big horn on the he-goat stands for Alexander the Great, who was able to move very swiftly in his capture of the Medo-Persian empire. However, Alexander the Great died at the early age of thirty-two and thus, at the zenith of his reign, the "big horn of the he-goat" was broken off. But Alexander had no children to leave his great Greek kingdom to.

So, when it says that in the place of the big horn grew "four notable ones" (Dan. 8:8), it describes how Alexander's great Greek kingdom was divided among his four generals, Ptolemy, Cassander, Lysimachus, and Seleucus I.

Then, out of one these horns (Seleucus I), another "little horn" grew which "waxed exceeding great". This "little horn", even though he is a foreshadow of that other "little horn" that will rule in last days of the iron/clay period, is not the same as that "little horn" described in Daniel 7:8, 24-26. This "little horn" that came from Seleucus I was **Antiochus Epiphanes**, the eighth in a long line of Seleucid kings, who became very powerful and was guilty of unbelievable atrocities against the Jews (the people of the "pleasant land").

70

So, in Daniel 8, Daniel is given some additional information about what would become of the empire of Alexander the Great. His great Greek empire would be divided into four sectors and out of one of them would come a man (Antiochus Epiphanes) who would stand out also as a "little horn" like the one in chapter 7 (Antichrist).

Short Summary

Let's stop and summarize briefly what God revealed to Daniel about the empires of "the Times of the Gentiles" of Nebuchadnezzar's dream.

1.   The gold head was representative of king Nebuchadnezzar and his **Babylonian** empire **(Gentile empire number one).**

2.   The Babylonians were defeated by the dual empire of the **Medes and Persians**, symbolized by the two arms and chest of silver **(Gentile empire number two).**

3.   The Persians (which was the dominant half of the Medo-Persian empire) were defeated in the remarkably swift campaigns of Alexander the Great of the nation of **Greece (Gentile empire number three).** For a couple of hundred years after the death of Alexander, the great empire of Greece was divided among his four generals and their descendants who constantly warred with one another.   One of the descendants of Alexander's general Seleucus I, was Antiochus Epiphanes, an especially cruel king that brought untold suffering to Israel. He is an OT picture of another "little horn" who is to rule in the final empire of the age… The Antichrist.

4.   Then, eventually the historic **Roman Empire** came to full power under Augustus around 31 BC **(Gentile empire number four)**

5.   This Roman Empire will eventually (one day) be revived in a weakened state represented by the feet of the statue in Nebuchadnezzar's dream that are made of a composite of iron and clay (two substances that do not mix).

So, there will be four great Gentile Empires that will dominate of the land of Palestine... followed by the revival of that fourth empire in a somewhat "weakened state". It will be the Revived Roman Empire... led initially by ten kings... and then by one supreme leader, the Antichrist.

6.   It is in the time of THAT empire that Jesus (The Rock) will come and destroy all of man's kingdoms and establish His Own everlasting kingdom.

The Antichrist's Rule

In Daniel 9:26, it is revealed to Daniel that "the prince that shall come" (the Antichrist) will confirm a covenant with many of the Jews for a period of seven years. But at the mid-point (3 ½ years into the covenant) he will break that covenant by entering into Jerusalem, stopping the sacrifices and oblations, and through the *"overspreading of abominations"*, he will cause the Temple to become desolate (empty).

Paul tells us in II Thess. 2 that he will oppose all that is called God and will exalt himself above all that is called God by sitting in the Temple and claiming to be God (II Thess. 2:4). We call this horribly sinful act of the Antichrist, "The Abomination of Desolation".

Daniel is also told in 9:26 that it is the people of this prince (the Antichrist) that will destroy the Temple and the city of Jerusalem. Again, we know that was the Romans (in 70 AD), so that's how we know that the last days empire of the Antichrist will be a Revived Roman Empire (along with the fact that last days Iron/Clay period is not spoken of as another or 5th empire, but as an extension of the fourth empire, the Roman Empire).

Is It Happening Now?

The big question that we want to answer is:
Is this great European Empire coming about today?
Are we seeing it develop right now... in our own lifetime?

If we look back at the last couple of thousand years of European history, we can see that the dream of uniting all of Europe into one nation has been around for a long time and several great leaders have tried to do it:

Charlemagne - 9th century
Napolean - 1800's under the French rule
Adolf Hitler – in the last century, under Nazi domination

But they all failed and the nations always went back to doing what they have always done… fighting and warring with one another.

However, in the last century, something happened that changed the entire picture in Europe… something that had never happened before… WWII.

After WWII, unlike any other time in all of history, Europe was devastated by the destruction of war. So, there was a desperate need for rebuilding after the war. This led to the voluntary cooperation by a few nations on certain **economic ventures** to be able to compete on the world market. Here's the basic scenario of how these economic treaties eventually turned into political treaties that have united the nations of Europe:

1951 - The European Coal and Steel Community (ECSC) was established. It was started by six nations – Belgium, France, W. Germany, Italy, Luxemburg, and The Netherlands

1957 - The Rome treaties were signed. Two additional commercial sectors were established to attain the same prosperity that the coal and steel companies were enjoying in the ECSC. They were the European Atomic Energy Community (Euratom, for the peaceful uses of nuclear energy) and the European Economic Community (EEC, which covered several areas of commerce).

1967 - These three treaties were fully merged to become the European Community (EC, also commonly called the European Common Market).

1973 - Three more nations were added to the group… Denmark, Ireland, and the United Kingdom bringing the total to 9 nations.

Late 1980's - Communism crumbled and Greece, Spain, and Portugal were added to the EC, bringing the total to 12 nations.

1991 - The Treaty on the European Union was adopted expanding their cooperation to political, and social integration. From this point on, it was no longer the European Community (EC), but the European Union (EU).

1995 - Austria, Finland, and Sweden joined the EU which brought the total member nations up to 15.

1997 - The Amsterdam Treaty was signed which among other things, provided for the removal of national barriers between member states.

May 1,2004 - Ten nations were added, the largest expansion at one time in history. Those nations were Czech Republic, Cyprus, Estonia, Latvia, Lithuania, Hungary, Malta, Poland, Slovenia, and Slovakia. This brought the total number of nations to 25.

June, 2004 – 63,000 word EU Constitution was accepted by the political leaders of the EU and submitted to the nations for each to ratify by public referendum. It was rejected by France and The Netherlands.

Jan. 1, 2007 - Romania and Bulgaria joined the EU bringing it to 27 nations with a population of 495 million.

Dec. 13, 2007 - The EU Constitution was revamped (but stayed about 95% the same) and resubmitted as the Reform Treaty for ratification by the legislatures of the member nations. A public vote was not required because it was now a "treaty" and not a constitution. It was passed and implemented on Dec. 1, 2009

Dec. 1, 2009 - The Reform Treaty, after passing in each of the member states, is implemented.

July 1, 2013 - Croatia was admitted as a member of the EU.

As of today (Jan. 1, 2015), there are 28 member nations in the European Union.

Is the European Union REALLY the Revived Roman Empire?

Look how far has the EU come in uniting the nations of Europe into one gigantic empire?

The EU has today:

> 1. All three departments for the functions of a federal government: Executive, Legislative, & Judicial
> 2. The power of taxation over the member states
> 3. A common currency called the Euro
> 4. The beginnings of a Police Force; It's called "The Rapid-Reaction Eurocorps" made up of 60,000 personnel

The member nations of the EU have already given up major portions of their sovereignty:

> 1. The European Court of Justice can overrule the highest court decisions in the member nations.
> 2. The European Parliament and European Council can legislate laws that all the member nations are forced to observe.
> 3. Member nations must pay 1.2% of their GDP as a tax to the EU.

The European Commission is the highest administrative department of the EU government. Presently, it has 28 commissioners… one for each member nation, one of which is the EC president. Presently, that man is **Jean-Claude Juncker.**

However, the new Reform Treaty, which was passed by the EU political leaders in 2008, stated initially that there would only be 15 commissioners instead of 27 (Croatia had not become a member at that time). But in the ratification process, out of the 27 member states of the EU, only Ireland required by its own constitution that the ratification be done by a public vote and it was initially voted down in Ireland. The major reason the Irish defeated the treaty was because of the reduction in the number of commissioners. No longer would there have been one commissioner for each nation. So, the EU took that section out of the treaty, leaving it as one commissioner for each nation. There was a revote in Ireland and it passed.

Even though the attempt of the European leadership to change the number of commissioners failed, for the first time, it is clear that they want to do away with the idea of one commissioner for each country. In their ongoing process of trying to eliminate nationalism, there is no doubt that they will eventually change the representation in the European Commission to some fewer number of commissioners. Will this eventually be reduced to ten????

For centuries, the nations of Europe have fought one another and all attempts to unite them into one "empire" have failed. But, in our lifetime, we have witnessed the European nations being integrated economically, socially, and politically under one government. Without a doubt, this is the new Revived Roman Empire (or, at least the beginnings of it) that Daniel 2 says will be the final empire of the age, through which the Antichrist will rise to power!

The official European motto is "Unity in Diversity". They make no apologies about their goal do UNDO what God did at the Tower of Babel. God scattered the people to form the nations. The EU is attempting to bring the nations together again… "Unity in Diversity".

The European Parliament in Strasburg, France includes a tower that appears to be unfinished. However, it was built this way by design to imitate the appearance of the Tower of Babel in the 1563 painting by Pieter Brueghel, a Flemish Northern Renaissance painter. This was NOT to commemorate the scattering of the nations, but just the opposite. It was built this way to make a statement that "God scattered the people. We are bringing them back together again."

The EU flag is blue with twelve stars on it in a circular pattern. This use of the 12 stars in a circle is inspired by the many Roman Catholic pictures of Mary with her halo of 12 stars (mistakenly identified with the woman in Revelation 12).

On June 23, 2007, the European Union published a very interesting poster showing Brueghel's Tower of Babel with the 12 stars of the EU flag above it. And behind the tower, there is a construction crane to show that they intend to rebuild the Tower of Babel. And the wording is "Europe: Many tongues, one voice."

But, the European symbolism of unity doesn't stop there! The Bible teaches in Revelation 17 that there will be a last days one-world religion and it is symbolically represented by a woman riding upon a beast.

Today, in front of the EU Parliament Building in Strasburg, France, there is a statue of a woman riding a beast. Also, the headquarters of the Council of Europe in Brussel has a bronze statue of a woman riding a beast, and the beast is shown riding on waves, just like in Rev. 17.

The Euro is the currency of the European Union. The 2 Euro coin in Greece has the engraving of the woman riding the beast.

Over and over again, this symbol of the woman riding the beast is used as a promotion of European unity. Even though the Europeans might explain that the symbol is taken from "Europa", a goddess of Greek mythology who is pictured riding upon a bull and from which the name of the continent is derived, it is still very interesting that the Bible used that same symbolism to denote the final one world empire and religion.

Perhaps the attitude of the modern European is best illustrated by the comments credited to Paul-Henri Spaak, the former Belgian Prime Minister from over 60 years ago. When the European Union was in its earliest stages of development, he supposedly said:

> "We do not want another committee. We have too many already. What we want is a man of sufficient stature to hold the allegiance of all people, and to lift us out of the economic morass in which we are sinking. Send us such a man and, be he God or the devil, we will receive him."

For those who have eyes to see it, the Bible is being fulfilled right before us. The new Revived Roman Empire which will eventually be ruled by ten kings who will give their power to the Antichrist… that last days empire that Jesus will destroy at His coming… also, the world ecumenical movement leading to the last days, one-world religion… **it's all here NOW!** Maybe we must admit that it's still in its developmental stages, but it is here. This tells me that we MUST be approaching the day when Jesus will come for His Church.

Are you ready?

Time of the Gentiles

Quiz

1. According to Daniel 2, King _____ had a dream of a _____ of a _____ whose:
   Head was _____
   Chest and arms were _____
   Stomach was _____
   Legs were _____
   Feet and toes were made of _____ and _____.

2. Daniel interpreted the king's dream to be symbolic of successive _____ empires and thus, we believe it is representative of the _____ of the _____.

3. The head of _____ was symbolic of the _____ Empire.
   The chest of _____ was symbolic of the _____ Empire.
   The stomach of _____ was symbolic of the _____ Empire.
   The legs of _____ were symbolic of _____ Empire.
   The feet of _____ and _____ were symbolic of a future Revived _____ Empire.

4. That last future empire will be ruled initially by a group of _____ men.

5. _____ will overthrow _____ of those men in his quest for power and then become the supreme leader of all ten.

6. These ten men will destroy the world ecclesiastical system and give their total allegiance to _____.

7. The _____ _____ of today appears to be the beginning of that future iron/clay empire.

8. The EU presently has _____ member nations with plans to add _____ more nations in the near future.

9. T or F   The European Union is strictly an economic union of nations.

10. T or F   Even if the EU become fully united as a single country, the United States will still be the most powerful nation on earth.

Time of the Gentiles
Quiz Answers

1. Nebuchadnezzar, statue, man
    gold
    silver
    brass
    iron
    iron, clay

2. gentile
    Time of the Gentiles

3. gold, Babylonian
    silver, Medo-Persian
    brass, Greek
    iron, Roman
    iron, clay, Roman

4. ten

5. Antichrist, three

6. Antichrist

7. European Union

8. 15, 12

9. False

10. False. The EU will exceed the United States in both population and economic measures (GNP).

Lesson 4

<u>The Antichrist and the Tribulation</u>

NOTE - This is a large topic, so keep in mind that this is a brief OVERVIEW of Bible Prophecy. Therefore, it is not possible for us to make a detailed study of the large subject matter of this lesson.

According to the Scriptures, there is coming a man who will step upon the international political scene who will possess unbelievable charisma, charm, and diplomatic persuasion. He will initially rise to power in Europe through peaceful (or at least "non-military") means and will head the most powerful multinational confederation that the world has ever seen. He will accomplish something that has been attempted by others for centuries that only resulted in consistent failure… He will bring peace to the Middle East.

For the first time in world history, this man will negotiate a treaty between Israel and all of her Arab neighbors that will give Israel a sense of peace and security and will even allow the next Jewish Temple to be built in Jerusalem. Such unprecedented diplomacy will catapult him to a place of highest respect, fame, and leadership in the hearts of people around the globe. Eventually, however, his methods will become much more sinister as he uses tightfisted economic regulation and a ruthless police force in an attempt to control the lives of every person on earth.

His insatiable appetite for the loyalty and adoration of the world's population will eventually move him to declare himself to be God, requiring everyone to worship him. This will happen at the same time that he breaks his treaty with Israel and begins to try to kill all Jews.

Toward the end of the Tribulation, he will begin to lose control of some of the nations who will rebel against him and he will meet them with a large army in northern Israel in the valley called Armageddon. At that time Jesus will return to earth in great power and glory. He will be resisted by this leader and the armies of earth, but the Lord will destroy them with "the sword of His mouth".

Then our Lord will cast this man and his most senior subordinate (called the False Prophet) into the everlasting lake of fire. Thus will be the end of this horrible man of evil… The Antichrist.

The Antichrist

In our study of this infamous "man of sin" called the Antichrist, we will begin by gleaning certain facts about him from the book of Daniel and the book of Revelation.

From the book of Daniel

Daniel records three separate visions given to him by God in chapters 7, 8, and 9 that we will use to learn about the Antichrist. Some of this has already been discussed in the previous lesson, so we will attempt to just pull individual facts from these chapters that relate to this man.

In Daniel 7, we have the vision of "The Four Beasts". The prophet sees four separate beasts coming up out of a turbulent sea in succession and he describes what each of them looks like.

The first looks like a lion with eagle's wings.
The second one looks like a bear that had three ribs in its mouth.
The third one looks like a leopard with four heads and four wings upon its back.
The fourth one did not look like any particular animal, but it was *"dreadful and terrible and strong exceedingly"* (Dan. 7:7). It had *"great iron teeth"* and *"ten horns"*.

As we discussed in the previous lesson, these four beasts represent four gentile empires that would rule over the land of Palestine (Israel) in history… (1) Babylonian, (2) Medo-Persian, (3) Greek, and (4) Roman.

As Daniel was looking at that terrible fourth beast, he noticed a "little horn" growing out of its skull among the ten horns. And as it came up, it uprooted three of the ten horns.

Dan. 7:8a - *I considered the horns, and, behold, there came up among them another little horn, before whom there were three of the first horns plucked up by the roots…*

Later, in the angelic interpretation given to Daniel about this, it says…

Dan. 7:24 - *And the ten horns out of this kingdom* [the fourth kingdom, the Revived Roman Empire] *are ten kings that shall arise; and another shall rise after them; and he shall be **diverse** from the first, and he shall subdue three kings.*

This "little horn", as previously discussed represents the Antichrist. So, the first fact that we learn about him is that…

1.   In his rise to power, he will overthrow three of the ten kings. As we will discuss later, his initial successes are through political maneuvering and his persuasive speech. Later in his political career, he will begin to use his military power to expand the borders of his empire. But at first, he achieves his purposes non-militarily.

2.   We also learn from this passage that he will be *"diverse from the first"* [first ten kings]. We can only guess about HOW he will be different from the ten kings that arise before him, but as we will learn, he will certainly be a man of exceptional talents. So, perhaps the meaning is that he will be **far superior** to the ten king… able to accomplish his goals with 100% success and able to outdo anyone who might oppose him.

Next, Daniel says that the "little horn" had some attributes of a person.

Daniel 7:8b - *…and, behold, in this horn were eyes like the eyes of man, and a mouth speaking great things.*

We read in Gen. 3:5 that when Satan tempted Eve to eat the forbidden fruit, that he said, *"For God doth know that in the day ye eat thereof, then **your eyes shall be opened**, and ye shall be as gods, knowing good and evil."* Here, Eve's the opening of Eve's eyes is an obvious reference to giving her knowledge. So,

3.   When the Scripture says that *"in this horn were eyes like the eyes of man"*, it is referring to the exceptional intellect that Antichrist will possess. In might also infer that he will be a *visionary* with great foresight.

Along with his superior intelligence, he will have *"a mouth speaking great things"*. So,

4.   Antichrist will be a great speaker.   His eloquence and persuasiveness of speech will serve him well in the political arena. First, it will help him in his rise to political greatness. Second, he will be able to convince the world that he has a plan and the power to restore order in the world of chaos after the Rapture. And thirdly, his speech will serve him well in negotiating a seven year peace treaty with Israel.

Later, in the interpretation part of the vision, Daniel says that the "little horn" had a *"look... more stout than his fellows"* (KJV).   The word translated here as "stout" means "great" or "imposing". So,

5.   Antichrist will have a very imposing demeanor, able to stare down his fellow politicians.

Daniel 7:21 - *I beheld, and the same horn made war with the saints, and prevailed against them.*

Vs. 25 says that he will *"wear out the saints of the most High"*. The "saints" is a reference to the believers, the followers of God.

Rev. 13:7a - *And it was given unto him to make war with the saints, and to overcome them...*

In Rev. 7:9, 14, a numberless multitude of the saints are seen by John standing before the throne of God in Heaven who *"came out of great tribulation"*. So, obviously MANY, MANY believers will die during the Tribulation and most of those will die at the hands of Antichrist. So,

6.   He will kill many of God's people.

Dan. 7:25a - *And he shall speak great words against the most High...*

Rev. 13:5a - *And there was given unto him a mouth speaking great things and blasphemies…*

7.   Among the many things that Antichrist will say, some of what he will say will be words against God in great blasphemy.

Dan. 7:25 says that he will *"think to change times and laws".* Most Bible scholars believe this is saying that

8.   He will attempt to change the Jewish observance of Sabbaths, Holy Days, and OT laws.

Dan. 7:25 also says that *"they shall be given into his hand until a time and times and the dividing of time."* The *"they"* here can refer to "the saints" and/or the Jews. The *"time and times and the dividing of time"* refers to 3 ½ years (the last half of the Tribulation).

Dan. 8:24b - *…and he shall destroy wonderfully, and shall prosper, and practice, and shall destroy the mighty **and the holy people**.*

In Rev. 12, *"the woman"* is a reference to the Jewish people.

Rev. 12:13 - *And when the dragon* [Satan, who will enter Antichrist] *saw that he was cast unto the earth, he persecuted the woman* [the Jewish people] *which brought forth the man child* [Jesus].
14   *And to the woman were given two wings of a great eagle, that she might fly into the wilderness, into her place, where she is nourished for a time, and times, and half a time, from the face of the serpent.*

9.   He will persecute and try to kill all Jews in the last half of the Tribulation.

Daniel 7:27 - *And the kingdom and dominion, and the greatness of the kingdom under the whole heaven shall be given to the people of the saints of the most High, whose kingdom is an everlasting kingdom, and all dominions shall serve and obey him.*

10. Ultimately, in the end, Antichrist will lose his kingdom and it will be given to God's people who will serve Jesus Christ.

In Daniel 8, the prophet is given the vision of "The Ram and the He-Goat" which also speaks of a "little horn". We discussed this in the last lesson, so not to be repetitious, but to serve as a reminder, the vision goes like this:

Daniel sees a very powerful ram standing next to the river Ulai that has two horns, one larger than the other. It was dominant *"so that no beasts might stand before him, neither was there an that cold deliver out of his hand"*. We said that this represents the Medo Persian Empire with the Persian side being the stronger half (the larger horn).

Suddenly, a he-goat with one large horn between his eyes came charging from the west and destroyed the ram. Then, the large horn on the he-goat was broken off and four other horns came up in its place. This is the Greek Empire led by Alexander the Great (the large horn) who died at an early age and his empire was divided to his four generals. And then, out of one of those four horns came another "little horn" that *"waxed exceeding great, toward the south, and toward the east, and toward the pleasant land* [the land of Palestine].*"* (Dan. 8:9) which we said is symbolic of the despot Antiochus Epiphanes who dealt great persecution to the Jewish people.

According to W.A. Criswell, "This little horn is Antiochus IV or Antiochus Epiphanes. He is the eighth in a long line of Seleucids who governed Syria from a capital at Antioch. This Antiochus ruled from 175 to 163 BC. As the "little horn", he should not be confused with the "little horn" of 7:8 who is the Antichrist of the end time. However, Antiochus is a type of the Antichrist. In bitter reprisal against the Jews, Antiochus attacked Jerusalem, killing fifty thousand men, women, and children. He sold an additional forty thousand people into slavery. The temple was dedicated to Jupiter Olympus, and on the great bronze altar a sow was offered, the juices of which were liberally spread throughout the temple precincts. He used harlots in the temple to celebrate Saturnalia [a celebration of the false deity Saturn] and forbade the observance of the Sabbath, the reading of Scripture, and circumcision. Verses 10-12 apparently refer to all of this. Small wonder that Antiochus was also called Epimanes, i.e., "Antiochus the madman." [1]

This is an unusual passage of Scripture in its arrangement.
Verses 9-14 deal with the vision of the "little horn" Antiochus Epiphanes.

Verses 15-22 deal with the interpretation of the vision given to Daniel, but it serves as a picture type of the other "little horn" in chapter 7, the Antichrist, for this is the main purpose of the vision, to tell Daniel about *"the time of the end"* (8:17) and *"the last end of the indignation"* (or, the end when the Tribulation will happen, 8:19).

Beginning in verse 23, the message jumps many centuries ahead to speak of the Antichrist.

Dan. 8:23 - *And in the latter time of their kingdom, when the transgressors are come to the full, a king of fierce countenance, and understanding dark sentences, shall stand up.*

So, we pick up here with the information given us about the Antichrist.

Dan. 8:24a - *And his power shall be mighty, but not by his own power...*

Rev. 13:2b - *...and the dragon gave his his power...*

11. Antichrist will receive his power from Satan.

Dan. 8:24b - *...and he shall destroy wonderfully, and shall **prosper**, and **practice** [thrive, succeed], and shall **destroy the mighty** and the holy people.*

12.   Along with his other success, he will prosper by even destroying the lives of great leaders.

Dan. 8:25a - *And through his policy also he shall cause **craft to prosper** in his hand...*

The word translated here as "craft" has nothing to do with commerce. It means "deceit". So, under his leadership, deception will abound.

13.   Under his leadership, deception will abound.

Dan. 8:25b - *...and he shall magnify himself in his heart...*

14.   He will be very egotistical and arrogant.

Dan. 8:25c - *...and by peace [he] shall destroy many...*

15.   Through his deception and political maneuvering (non-military means), he will destroy anyone who gets in his way.

In Daniel 9, we learn about a horrible thing that Antichrist will do.

Dan. 9:27 - *And he shall confirm the **covenant** with **many** for **one week**; and in the midst of the week he shall cause the sacrifice and the oblation to cease, and for the overspreading of abominations, he shall make it desolate even until the consummation, and that determined shall be poured upon the desolate.*

Most Bible scholars believe that this covenant will be a **peace treaty** where Antichrist will guarantee safety to Israel. In light of the history of modern Israel, this certainly makes sense because this is the one thing that she has wanted, but has been unable to acquire since her founding in 1948. It may also include giving the Jews the right to rebuild their temple on the Temple Mount in Jerusalem

Because we know that this whole chapter deals with Daniel's people, the Jews, (Dan. 9:5-16, notice Daniel's use of the words *we* and *us*, and *thy people* in 9:24), the *"many"* that Antichrist confirms the covenant with are many of the Jewish people, Israel.

The use of the word *"week"* refers to a period of seven, which in this case is a reference to seven years. It is a seven year treaty. Perhaps, it will be promoted as a seven year "trial period" of the agreements of the covenant.

16.   Antichrist will make a seven year treaty with Israel guaranteeing her protection and possibly giving them the right to build the Temple in Jerusalem.

The *"midst of the week"* would be half way (3 ½ years) into it. At that time, he will *"cause the sacrifice and the oblation to cease"* making the Temple *"desolate"* until the end of the Tribulation. Most likely, the *"abomination"* referred to here is an image of himself that he will set up in the Temple and require people to bow down to it (Rev. 13:14-15).

2 Thess. 2:4 - *Who* [talking about the Antichrist] *opposeth and exalteth himself above all that is called God, or that is worshipped; so that he as God sitteth in the temple of God, showing himself that he is God.*

Through this overspreading sin, he will make the Temple empty (no worshippers of God) until the end of the Tribulation. This awful act is referred to as **The Abomination of Desolation.**

17.   At the mid-point of the seven-year Tribulation, Antichrist will take control of the Temple in Jerusalem and stop all the Jewish sacrifices. He will have an image of himself put in the Temple and require all people to worship him.

In Revelation 13, the Apostle John sees a vision of a beast coming up out of the sea that he describes as having seven heads and ten horns. The make-up of its body was like a **leopard**, but it had feet like a **bear** and a mouth like a **lion**.

Rev. 13:1 - *And I stood upon the sand of the sea and saw a beast rise up out of the sea, having **seven heads** and **ten horns**, and upon his horns ten crowns, and upon his heads the name of blasphemy.*
*2   And the beast which I saw was like unto a **leopard,** and his feet were as the feet of a **bear**, and his mouth as the mouth of a **lion**: and the dragon gave him his power, and his seat, and great authority.*

This beast represents both the Antichrist and his empire, which will ultimately be a composite of the same four empires represented in Daniel's vision of the four great beasts in Daniel 7.

Remember that the four beasts in Daniel 7 were:
1.   A lion with wings
2.   A bear
3.   A four-headed leopard with wings
4.   A monster beast with ten horns

If we combine these four beasts into one, notice what we would have:
A beast that looks partly like a lion, partly like a bear, and partly like a leopard. It would have seven heads (**one** like a lion + **one** like a bear + **four** like a leopard + **one** like a monster = seven heads). And the monster head would have ten horns on it.

This is what John saw in Rev. 13… a composite beast of Daniel 7.

18.   The Antichrist and the basic part of his empire will encompass all that the empires of the Babylonians, Medo-Persians, Greeks, and Romans encompassed (territorially, politically, economically, and militarily) even though he will eventually for a short time have control over the entire planet.

Rev. 13:7b - *…and power was given him over all kindreds, and tongues, and nations.*

Rev. 13:3 tells us that one of the heads (presumably the monster head) was wounded and appeared to die, but revived.

Rev. 13:3 - *And I saw one of his heads **as it were** wounded to death; and his deadly wound was healed; and all the world wondered after the beast.*

Rev. 13:14b - *...he* [the False Prophet]...*saying to them that dwell on the earth, that they should make an image to the beast* [Antichrist], ***which had a wound by a sword and did live.***

19.   Through an assassination attempt on the Antichrist, he will appear to die, but then will come back to life. This will be Satan's imitation of the death, burial, and resurrection of Christ.

Rev. 13:4 - *And they worshipped the dragon which gave power unto the beast; and they worshipped the beast, saying, Who is like unto the beast? Who is able to make war with him?*

20.   The world will be amazed at the seemingly supernatural power of the Antichrist and will worship and admire both him and Satan.

The seemingly unstoppable success of Antichrist, along with his great talents for deception, will appear to be supernatural. People will think that no mere man could possibly do the things that he does. And so, all those who are not born of the Spirit of God will worship him.

Rev. 13:8 - *And all that dwell upon the earth shall worship him, whose names are not written in the book of life of the Lamb slain from the foundation of the world.*

21.   Eventually, the people of the whole world who are not saved will worship Antichrist.

But at the end of the seven-year Tribulation, Jesus Christ will return in great power and glory to defeat the enemies of God and establish His Millennial Kingdom on earth. He will be met by the Antichrist and his armies, but they won't have a chance as King Jesus destroys them with the sword of His mouth.

Rev. 19:19 - *And I saw the beast, and the kings of the earth, and their armies, gathered together to make war against him that sat on the horse* [King Jesus], *and against his army.*

20 *And the beast was taken, and with him the false prophet that wrought miracles before him, with which he deceived them that had received the mark of the beast, and them that worshipped his image. **These both were cast alive into a lake of fire burning with brimstone.***

21 *And the remnant were slain with the sword of him that sat upon the horse, which sword proceedeth out of his mouth; and all the fowls were filled with their flesh.*

22. Jesus will come at the end of the Tribulation and destroy the armies of the Antichrist and all those who oppose Him. He will then throw Antichrist and the False Prophet into the lake of fire... their eternal habitation.

Thus will the end be for the Man of Sin, the Antichrist.

The Tribulation

Entire books have been written about The Tribulation. Obviously, we don't have space in this lesson series to cover even a small part of that information. However, there are a few main points that I will make about "Daniel's Seventieth Week" (The Tribulation).

Most people want to know first of all WHY God is going to do this.

If God is a God of love... and He loves people... why would he inflict such unimaginable pain and suffering on humanity? Daniel gives us the answer.

In Daniel 9, we find the prophet praying to God for forgiveness of the sin of his people (the Jews) and asking that God restore them to their homeland, allow them to rebuild their holy city Jerusalem and the Temple. But God tells Daniel that (even though the Babylonian captivity is almost over) the He was going to deal with Daniel's people for another 490 years! And then He tells him WHY.

Dan. 9:24 - *Seventy weeks are determined upon thy people and upon thy holy city, to finish the transgression, and to make an end of sins, and to make reconciliation for iniquity, and to bring in everlasting righteousness, and to seal up the vision and prophecy, and to anoint the most Holy.*

God said that He had determined to deal with Daniel's people for another 70 "weeks" which literally mean another 70 periods of 7. In this case, it refers to 7 years. So, it would be 70 x 7 years = 490 years.

Then, He gives six reasons for doing this. We won't take time to look at all six reasons, but let's take a look at just two of them:

> **1.** **"To finish the transgression"** - Israel is still to this day in transgression against God. They are nation of unbelievers who have rejected their Messiah, Jesus Christ and their transgressions against God will not be finished until they as a nation repent and turn to God at the end of the Tribulation.

> **2.** **"To bring in everlasting righteousness"** - Certainly, the Jews nor anyone else on this earth have begun to experience everlasting righteousness. That will only happen when the Lord's earthly kingdom is established.

So, if I were to sum up the six reasons that God gives for the seventy weeks of years that He said He was going to deal with Daniel's people, I would say it this way:

> He is going to use this time to allow Israel to complete their sinful path, at which time, He is going to bring their sins to an end and make reconciliation with them. After that, He will usher in a new era of everlasting righteousness, bringing to and end all of the visions and prophecies that He said He would fulfill. This will be finally celebrated by His presence in the Holy of Holies of the Temple from where He will reign over the world.

Another more concise summary could be this:

> God is going to bring the Jewish people to the end of themselves so that they will, in final desperation, turn to Christ and be saved.

Next, most folks want to know HOW we know the Tribulation is going to last just seven years.

In Daniel 9:25-27, the seventy weeks of years are divided into three groups:

<pre>
7 weeks = 7 x 7 =   49 years
62 weeks = 62 x 7 = 434 years
1 week   = 1 x 7 =   7 years
            Total =   490 years
</pre>

Verse 25 tells us when the countdown on the 490 will start:

Dan. 9:25 - *Know therefore and understand, that from the going forth of the commandment to restore and build Jerusalem unto the Missiah the Prince shall be seven weeks, and threescore and two weeks...*

So, from the time the decree was made for the Jews to return to their land to *"build Jerusalem"*, God's stopwatch started on the 490 years. There were actually four decrees made for the Jews to return to Jerusalem, but the first three only gave them permission to rebuild the Temple. It was the Persian king Artaxerxes who gave Nehemiah permission to return and **rebuild the city walls**.

Nehemiah 2:1 - *And it came to pass in the month of Nisan, in the twentieth year of Artaxerxes the king* [April, 445 BC], *that wine was before him; and I took up the wine, and gave it unto the king. Now I had not been beforetime sad in his presence...*

5 *And I said unto the king, If it please the king, and if thy servant have found favor in thy sight, that thous wouldest send me unto Judah, unto the city of my fathers' sepulchers, that I may build it.*

6 *...So it pleased the king to send me; and I set him a time.*

Daniel 9:26 tells us that after the 62 week of years segment, that the Messiah would be killed.

Dan. 9:26a - *And after* [the] *threescore and two weeks shall Messiah be cut off, but not for himself...*

Look at the accuracy of God's Word! Consider this calculation from the time Artaxerxes gave Nehemiah permission to rebuild the city until the time Jesus was crucified and see how it is exactly 483 years (the 7 weeks + the 62 weeks = 69 weeks   69 x 7 = 483 years).

First, there are two things we have to understand:

1.   We begin by understanding that a "Bible Year" is a little different from our Gregorian calendar year. A Bible Year = 360 days (12 months of 30 days each, see Gen. 7:11 – 8:4). And of course, our calendar year is 365.25 days long.

2.   Next, we must understand that there was never a year "0" on our calendar. When we went from 1 BC to 1 AD, it was considered just one year, even though on the time line, it would have to be two years. So, we lost one year in the BC to AD crossover.

So, starting in 445 BC, the prophecy says there would be 483 years until Messiah would die. But that is in Bible Years. So to convert it to our calendar years...

    483 Bible years x 360 days per year = 173,880 days

    173,880 days divided by 365.25 days per cal. year = 476 cal. Yrs.

    Moving from 446 BC ahead 476 years brings us to the year 31 AD.

    But 31 AD minus 1 year for the BC/AD crossover = 30 AD
    Which is the year most scholars believe Jesus was crucified!

You will remember, of course, how the Jews rejected Jesus as their Messiah and crucified Him. So, after the first two segments of years were complete and Jesus was crucified, God stopped His clock of dealing with Daniel's people and turned His attention the Gentile nations to gather out this special group of people called The Church... or, the Bride of Christ.

In this Age of Grace in which we now live, the whole Church is being formed. And when the very last person who is going to be saved is born again into the body of Christ, the Bride will be complete and the Groom (Jesus) will come for His Bride (the Rapture).

Then God will turn His attention back to Daniel's people to complete that last seven years of the 490 years that He said He was going to deal with them. **THAT SEVEN YEARS** is the seven-year Tribulation... or, as some call it, Daniel's Seventieth Week.

And THAT is how we know the Tribulation will last seven years of 360 days each, or a total of 2520 days!

The main purpose of the Tribulation is to complete God's dealing with Daniel's people. And even though it will also be a horrible day of judgment on all the sinful people of earth, it's mostly about what God is going to be doing to the Jews to bring them to the end of themselves and to bring a remnant of them into an everlasting salvation in Christ Jesus.

So, remember!
The Tribulation is not about the Church. It's not FOR the Church. It's about God's dealing with the Jews! The Church won't be here! Hallelujah!

There are many events described for us in the book of Revelation about the time of the Tribulation which we don't have space here to discuss. However, here is

A Brief Outline of the Tribulation and Beyond in The Book of Revelation

1. **The Seven Seal Judgments**

    First Seal – A White Horse (Rev. 6:1-2)
    Second Seal – A Red Horse (Rev. 6:3-4)
    Third Seal – A Black Horse (Rev. 6:5-6)
    Fourth Seal – A Pale Horse (Rev. 6:7-8)

Fifth Seal – Souls of Martyrs (Rev. 6:9-11)
Sixth Seal – Physical Changes (Rev. 6:12-17)

Interval between sixth and seventh seal judgments
      (1)   Sealing of 144,000 Jews (Rev. 7:1-8)
      (2)   Blood washed multitude (Rev. 7:9-17)

Seventh Seal – Silence (Rev. 8:1) and the Golden Censer (Rev. 8:3-5)

2.   The Seven Trumpet Judgments

First Trumpet – Hail, fire, and blood (Rev. 8:7)
Second Trumpet – Burning mountain (Rev. 8:8-9)
Third Trumpet – Star Wormwood (Rev. 8:10-11)
Fourth Trumpet – Sun, moon, and stars smitten (Rev. 8:12)

Angel warns of "Three Woes" (Rev. 8:13)

Fifth Trumpet (First Woe) – Plague of locust demons (Rev. 9:1-12)
Sixth Trumpet (Second Woe) – Plague of horsemen (Rev. 9:13-21)

Interval between sixth and seventh trumpet judgments
      (1)   Little Book (Rev. 10:1-11)
      (2)   Two Witnesses (Rev. 11:1-14)

Seventh Trumpet (Third Woe) – Covers the remainder of the week (Rev. 11:15-20:10) and includes:
      (1)   Seven Personages
      (2)   Seven Vials
      (3)   Four dooms

3.   The Seven Individuals

First Individual – The Sun-clothed Woman (Rev. 12:1-2)
Second Individual – The Dragon (Rev. 12:3-4)
Third Individual – The Man-Child (Rev. 12:5-6)
Fourth Individual – The Archangel (Rev. 12:7-12)

Fifth Individual – The Jewish Remnant (Rev. 12:13-17)
Sixth Individual – The Beast out of the sea (Antichrist) (Rev. 13:1-10)
Seventh Individual – The Beast out of the earth (False Prophet) (Rev. 13:11-18)

4.   **The Seven Vial (Bowl) Judgments**

   Prelude (Rev. 15:1)
       (1)   The Sea of Glass (Rev. 15:2-4)
       (2)   The Tabernacle of Testimony (Rev. 15:5-8)

   First Vial – Boils (Rev. 16:1-2)
   Second Vial – Blood on the sea (Rev. 16:3)
   Third Vial – Blood on the rivers (Rev. 16:4-7)
   Fourth Vial – Great heat (Rev. 16:8-9)
   Fifth Vial – Darkness (Rev. 16:10-11)
   Sixth Vial – Euphrates River dried up (Rev. 16:12)

Interval between sixth and seventh vial judgments
    Three unclean spirits released (Rev. 16:13-16)

Seventh Vial – Great Hail (Rev. 16:17-21)

5.   **The Seven Dooms (first two happen during Tribulation)**

   First Doom – Destruction of Ecclesiastical Babylon (Rev. 17:1-18)
   Second Doom – Destruction of Commercial Babylon (Rev. 18:1-24)

Interval between second and third dooms
    (1)   The Hallelujah Chorus (Rev. 19:1-7)
    (2)   The Marriage of the Lamb (Rev. 19:8-10)
    (3)   The Battle of Armageddon (Rev. 19:11-21)

   Third Doom – Destruction of Antichrist and the False Prophet (Rev. 19:20)
   Fourth Doom – Destruction of Antichrist Armies (Rev. 19:21)

Interval between fourth and fifth doom
   (1) Satan bound (Rev. 20:1-3)
   (2) First Resurrection (Rev. 20:4-5)
   (3) The Millennium (Rev. 20:6)
   (4) Satan Loosed (Rev. 20:7)

Fifth Doom – Gog and Magog (Rev. 20:8-9)
Sixth Doom – Satan destroyed (Rev. 20:10)
Seventh Doom – The wicked dead judged at the Great White Throne Judgments (Rev. 20:11-15)

In the last two chapters of Revelation, there are SEVEN NEW THINGS presented:
(1) The New Heaven
(2) The New Earth
(3) The New City
(4) The New Nations
(5) The New River
(6) The New Tree
(7) The New Throne

(1) W.A. Criswell, *The Criswell Study Bible,* (Nashville, Camden, and New York: Thomas Nelson, 1979) page 992

Antichrist and the Tribulation
Quiz

1. In both Daniel's visions of "the four beasts" and "the ram and the he-goat", the Antichrist is symbolically represented by a _____ _____.

2. According to Daniel 7:8, one of Antichrist's greatest abilities is his ability of _____ because it says he has a mouth _____ _____ _____.

3. In Daniel 7:25, it says that he will _____ God, he will _____ _____ the saints, and he will try to change the _____ and _____ (of the Jewish people) for _____ years.

4. In Daniel's vision of the ram and he-goat (chapter 8), the "notable horn" on the he-goat was symbolic of _____ ____ _____.

5. _____ _____ appears to be an Old Testament "type" of the Antichrist because of the way he persecuted the Jews and desecrated their Temple in Jerusalem.

6. In Daniel 9:27, it says that Antichrist will desecrate the Temple with an "overspreading of abominations". This will happen _____ years into the Tribulation and it is called the _____ ____ _____.

7. T or F   According to Revelation 13, the Antichrist receives a deadly wound, but he revives from it.

8. T or F   According to Rev. 13:7, Antichrist will eventually rule the entire world.

9. In Daniel 9:24-27, the term "week" actually means "period of seven" and we believe it to refer to a period of seven _____.

10. The term "Daniel's Seventieth Week" refers to the period we most often refer to as the _____.

Antichrist and the Tribulation
Quiz Answers

1.   little horn

2.   speech, "speaking great things"

3.   blaspheme, wear out, times and laws, 3 ½

4.   Alexander the Great

5.   Antiochus Epiphanes

6.   3 ½, Abomination of Desolation

7.   True

8.   True

9.   years

10.   Tribulation

Lesson 5

The Millennial Kingdom

According to the Scriptures, our Lord Jesus Christ will return to earth at the end of (or after) The Tribulation. He will defeat His enemies at Armageddon (Rev. 16:16, 19:11-21) and judge the remaining people in the valley of Jehoshaphat (Joel 3:1-2, Matt. 25:31-46) at the "Judgment of Nations" to determine who is worthy to enter His kingdom. He will then establish His earthly, visible, literal kingdom in which He will rule in peace, justice, and righteousness for one thousand years. We call this time **"The Millennial Kingdom"**.

NOTE - As in the previous lesson on the Antichrist, we will attempt to provide some Biblical facts about the "Millennium" that will give the student an overall picture of what it is and what it will be like, along with some commentary from the author.

1.   The Millennial Kingdom will last for one thousand years.

The word "millennium" comes from two Latin words:
>   "mille" meaning thousand
>   "annum" meaning year
Thus, together we have the "millennium" meaning "a thousand years"

Note - In this lesson, I will sometimes use the word "Millennium" in place of the words "Millennial Kingdom".

In John's discussion of the time period of the Millennium in Rev. 20, he speaks of the time of "1000 years" **six times**, once in each verse from Rev. 20:2-7. Some would have us to believe that this number shouldn't be taken literally, but that it is only **symbolic** language of a "very long time". However, without entering the debate about why it is so important to **always** take the Scriptures **LITERALLY** except when it is obvious that it is symbolic, metaphorical, or analogical, it seems very obvious through John's repetitive use of the number 1000, that he meant exactly that! **The Millennial Kingdom will be for 1000 years.**

Note also that when Peter wrote *"But beloved, be not ignorant of this one thing, that one day is with the Lord as a thousand years, and a thousand years as one day"* (2 Peter 3:8), he could have been speaking more literally more than metaphorically about the "meaninglessness of time" to our infinite God. Many early Church fathers believed that God would deal with mankind for six one thousand year periods (4000 before Christ and 2000 after Christ) and then, He would enjoy another 1000 years of rest on this earth (the Millennium) for a total of 7000 years... just like the 7 days of the creation week when on the seventh day He rested from His creation work. This may certainly have some validity to it, but only time will tell. (By the way, because of the imperfections in our Gregorian calendar system, you can't use its dates for calculating when we've reached the 6000th year.) If this idea of the 7000 years of mankind is valid, then obviously the literal 1000 Millennium is essential.

2.   The Millennial Kingdom will start AFTER the Second Coming of Jesus Christ.

There are three main views about the timing of the Lord's Second Coming relative to the Millennial Kingdom:

1.   Premillennial - The Lord will come BEFORE the start of the Millennium.
2.   Postmillennial - The Lord will come AFTER the Millennium.
3.   Amillennial - There will be no Millennium.

The detailed explanation of these three positions and their Scriptural validity is beyond the scope of this lesson. However, suffice it to say that his author believes that the Premillennial viewpoint is the correct one. And, there are just a couple of points that I would like to make in that respect.

1.   There is much said about the Millennial Kingdom in the Bible by the OT prophets. In fact, it is a major theme of their prophecies because they so longed for the coming of their Messiah and the establishment of His kingdom. However, they could not see the vast time period that would exist between our Lord's First Coming and His Second Coming.
Let me explain...

From the OT Scriptures, they could recognize the many details prophesied about the Messiah… information about His birth, His genealogy, His life, His reign, and His Kingdom.

If you can picture this… As they looked forward in time to the coming of their Messiah, they saw all that Messianic information as **a single mountain peak**. What they COULD NOT understand was that they were looking at TWO mountain peaks with a great valley of time in between them.

The first "mountain peak" of information (His First Advent) was all that information that dealt with things like His birth, His life, etc. They chose to ignore the prophecies about His death because that would be against their beliefs about Him coming to establish His *eternal* kingdom. The second mountain peak of information dealt with His glorious reign as the King of kings and His great kingdom. They saw both mountain peaks as one!

But we know that at the conclusion of His First Advent, He was crucified, resurrected, and ascended into Heaven. And then, on Pentecost, He inaugurated The Church Age, that great "valley" of time BETWEEN the mountain peak of information concerning His First Coming and the mountain peak of information about His Second Coming.

From where we are in history today (in that valley between His two comings), it is easy for us to distinguish between the information related to His two comings as we look BACK at the prophecies already fulfilled at His First Coming and look FORWARD to the prophecies about His Second Coming. But had we lived in the OT times, looking forward to the coming of the Messiah (like the OT prophets), it would have been much harder to recognize how the time of the Church Age (already almost 2000 years) would fall in between the TWO comings of the Messiah.

With all of that being said, we can better understand the OT prophecies about the Millennial Kingdom when we look at them with the realization of how the OT prophets viewed the coming of their Messiah.

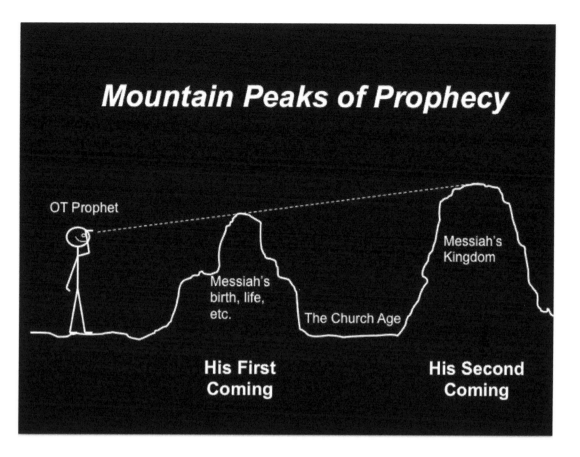

Mountain Peaks of Prophecy

OT Prophet

Messiah's birth, life, etc.

The Church Age

Messiah's Kingdom

His First Coming

His Second Coming

2. The other thing we must understand is that all of the OT prophecies about the coming Messianic Kingdom are given from "the Jewish perspective". That is, their hope and dream was for the Messiah to come and establish Israel as the head of all nations. And certainly, He will do that. But most Millennial Kingdom prophecies speak to what a glorious day that that is going to be fore THE JEWS! We know, of course, that God's plan for the Church (which is mostly Gentiles) is even MORE glorious. So, even though the OT prophecies speak mostly of what wonderful day the Millennium will be for the Jews, we can extrapolate a lot of that information and add it to the NT prophecies to understand what will be happening with all of mankind in the Millennium, which brings us to our next point…

3. All born again believers of The Church will be immortal during the Millennial Kingdom.

Remember, **_all_** Christians will be called up to Heaven in the Rapture before the Tribulation begins. Some (those who will have died before the Rapture) will have their new, immortal bodies resurrected from the grave to join with their eternal soul and spirit when they come with the Lord. And the rest (those who will still be alive at the Rapture) will receive their new glorified bodies on the way up to meet the Lord in the air.

1 Thess. 4:16 - *For the Lord himself shall descend from heaven with a shout, with the voice of the archangel, and with the trump of God; and **the dead in Christ shall rise first;***
17 ***Then we which are alive and remain shall be caught up together with them in the clouds**, to meet the Lord in the air; and so shall we ever be with the Lord."*

So, in that translation, **_all_** of us Christians of the Church Age will receive our new, immortal body.

1 Cor. 15:51 - *Behold, I show you a mystery; We shall not all sleep* [die], *but we shall **all** [both the dead and the living] be changed.*
52 *In a moment, in the twinkling of an eye, at the last trump; for the trumpet shall sound, and the dead shall be raised incorruptible, and we* [who are still alive] *shall be changed.*

So, during the Tribulation, we Christians of the Church Age will be in Heaven with our Lord Jesus enjoying the Marriage Feast of the Lamb (Rev. 19:6-9). Then, when the Lord returns to the earth at the end of the Tribulation, at His Second Coming, we Christians will return with Him (Zech. 14:5, Col. 3:4, I Thess. 3:13, Jude 14) as ***"immortals"*** to reign with Him in His kingdom.

Col. 3:4 - *When Christ, who is our life, shall appear, **then shall ye also appear with him in glory**.*

1 Thess. 3:13 - *To the end he may stablish your hearts unblamable in holiness before God, even our Father, at the coming of our Lord Jesus Christ **with all his saints**.*

Rev. 20:6 - *Blessed and holy is he that hath part in the first resurrection: on such the second death hath no power, but they shall be priests of God and of Christ **and shall reign with him a thousand years**.*

4.   There will also be mortal people living on earth during the Tribulation.

Not all people on earth will die during the Tribulation. Even though the book of Revelation indicates that over half of the earth's population will die during the Tribulation from all the war, famine, plagues, and persecution, there will still be some who manage to survive its horrors. Most of those will be people who chose to take the mark of the beast and follow the Antichrist. But a few will be those who chose to NOT give their loyalty to the Antichrist and miraculously managed to survive by hiding from him.

So, all those who are still living will be judged by Jesus at the "Judgment of Nations" in the valley of Jehoshaphat (Joel 3:1-2, Matt. 25:31-46) to determine who will enter the Lord's kingdom. According to Jewish tradition, the valley of Jehoshaphat is that part of the upper Kidron valley between the Temple Mount and the Mount of Olives.

Joel 3:1-2 - *For, behold, in those days, and in that time, when I shall bring again the captivity of Judah and Jerusalem,*
2   I will also gather all nations, and will bring them down into the valley of Jehoshaphat, and will plead with them there for my people and for my heritage Israel, whom they have scattered among the nations, and parted my land.

Matt. 25:31 - *When the Son of man shall come in his glory, and all the holy angels with him, then shall he sit upon the throne of his glory;*
32   And before him shall be gathered all nations; and he shall separate them one from another, as a shepherd divideth his sheep from the goats:
33   And he shall set the sheep on his right hand, but the goats on the left.
34   Then shall the King say unto them on his right hand, Come, ye blessed of my Father, inherit the kingdom prepared for you from the foundation of the world.

41   Then shall he say also unto them on the left hand, Depart from me, ye cursed, into everlasting fire, prepared for the devil and his angels.

46   And these shall go away into everlasting punishment: but the righteous into life eternal.

5.   At the end of the Tribulation, before the Millennial Kingdom starts, Satan will be locked up in the bottomless pit.

Although the Millennial Kingdom will not be a time of perfect sinlessness (Rev. 20:7-9) because mortal humans will be in it, it WILL be a time without the direct influence of Satan.

Rev. 20:1 - And I saw an angel come down from heaven, having the key of the bottomless pit and a great chain in his hand.
2   And he laid hold on the dragon, that old serpent, which is the Devil, and Satan, and bound him a thousand years.
3   And cast him into the bottomless pit, and shut him up, and set a seal upon him, that he should deceive the nations no more till the thousand years should be fulfilled: and after that he must be loosed a little season.

What a wonderful blessing it will be for the citizens of the Millennial Kingdom to not be tempted by the wickedness of Satan. His personal, evil influence will be totally removed at that time. But it will not be a perfect time of sinlessness because there will still be mortal human beings living in that time who will have to deal with the sins of their flesh (greed, lust, pride, etc.). Consequently,

6.   Sin will still exist during the Millennial Kingdom.

The Millennium will not be a **perfect** time, as it will be in the eternal ages of the new Heaven and new Earth. Even though King Jesus will rule the nations with a "rod of iron" (Rev. 19:15), and for the most part, everyone will live in obedience to His commandments, deep within the hearts of some individual, there will be a "seething" to overthrow His rule and live without His constant oversight. We see this come to light at the end of the Millennium when Satan will be loosed for a short season. He will go out and deceive millions of people in the nations into rebelling against King Jesus. However, DURING the thousand years of the Millennium…

7.   It will be a time of worldwide PEACE.

All wars will cease and there will be no more militaries. Thus, all the expense and energy that was previously devoted to armies and weapons will be redirected toward agricultural and industrial efforts, which will result in tremendous economic prosperity. This is a major theme of the OT prophets when talking about the Messiah's kingdom.

Isa. 2:4 - *And he shall judge among the nations, and shall rebuke many people: and they shall beat their swords into plowshares, and their spears into pruninghooks; **nation shall not lift up sword against nation, neither shall they learn war any more**.*

Isa. 32:17 - *And the work of righteousness shall be **peace***; *and the effect of righteousness quietness and assurance for ever.*
*18   And my people shall dwell in a **peaceable** habitation, and in sure dwellings, and in quiet resting places;*

(See also Isa. 9:6-7, 14:7-8, 33:5-6, 54:13, 55:12, 60:18, 65:25, 66:12, Ezek. 28:26, Hosea 2:18, Micah 4:3, Zech. 9:10)

8.   It will be a time of great JOY.

Overall, the people of earth will live in a mood of **joy**. Think of that. People everywhere will be singing, laughing, smiling and enjoying pleasant conversation. There will be no arguing, fighting, or scowling expressions. Everyone you meet will be polite, courteous, and pleasant. JOY will fill everyone's heart (for the most part).

Isa. 12:3 - *Therefore with **joy** shall ye draw water out of the wells of salvation.*
*4   And in that day shall ye say, **Praise the Lord**, call upon His name, declare His doings among the people, make mention that His name is exalted.*
*5   **Sing** unto the Lord; for He hath done excellent things; this is known in all the earth.*
6   Cry out and shout, thou inhabitant of Zion; for great is the Holy One of Israel in the midst of thee.

Zech. 10:6 - *And I will strengthen the house of Judah, and I will save the house of Joseph, and I will bring them again to place them; for I have mercy upon them; and they shall be as though I had not cast them off; for I am the Lord their God, and will hear them.*

*7   And they of Ephraim shall be like a mighty man, and **their heart shall rejoice as through wine**; yea, their children shall see it, and be glad; their heart shall rejoice in the Lord.*

(See also Isa. 25:8-9, 42:10-12, 52:9, 60:15, 61:10, 65:18-19, 66:10-14, Jer. 30:18-19 31:13-14, Zeph. 3:14-15)

9.   HOLINESS will be the norm throughout the whole world.

Perhaps the best synonym of the word "holy" is "god-like" because God is holy (Psa. 22:3). And because God is also righteous, and just, and fair, and kind, and loving, and possessed a thousand other such attributes, it is almost impossible to imagine the people of this world being holy (like God). But the Bible is clear that the people of the Millennium will possess these many god-like qualities.

Again, this is a general expression of how people will because remember, it is not a perfect time and men will still be controlled by their mortal flesh. So, even though there may still be some signs of sadness or irritability from time to time, that will certainly not be the norm and will stand out as "out of place".

Joel 3:21 - *For I will cleanse their blood* [change what they're made of] *that I have not cleansed; for the Lord dwelleth in Zion.*

Isa. 60:21a - *Thy people also shall be all righteous…*

(See also Isa. 4:3-4, 31:7, 35:8-9, Jer. 31:23, Ezek. 36:24-31, 37:23, Zeph. 3:11, Zech. 13:1-2, 14:20-21)

10.   The GLORY of the Lord will cause the beauty of nature in the kingdom to shine.

After the overwhelming destruction of the Tribulation, planet earth will be a charred planet. Most of the beauty of nature will be gone after the destruction of all the wars and divine plagues. But the Lord will restore the planet to its Edenic beauty with beautiful forests, lush grasslands and abundant wildlife. Then, it will be His glory that makes the grass and leaves a vibrant green, the waters a crystal clear blue, and all the colors of nature extraordinarily vivid.

Isa. 35:1 - *The wilderness and the solitary place shall be glad for them; and the desert shall rejoice, and blossom as the rose.*
2 *It shall blossom abundantly, and rejoice even with joy and singing; the glory of Lebanon shall be given unto it, the excellency of Carmel and Sharon, they shall see the glory of the Lord, and the excellency of our God.*

(See also Isa. 24:23, 4:2, 40:5, 60:1-2)

11. King Jesus will minister to every need so that there will be COMFORT in the lives of all His people.

People will labor, but it will be a joy and give great satisfaction. No longer will people sweat and be burdened with hard labor. So, even while people perform their jobs, they will be done in comfort. There won't be any back breaking, hard, manual labor. The curse of hard labor that God put on Adam when he sinned (Gen. 3:17-19) will be removed.

Isa. 12:1 - *And in that day, thou shalt say, O Lord, I will praise thee: though thou was angry with me, thine anger is turned away, and thou comfortedst me.*
2 *Behold, God is my salvation: I will trust, and not be afraid: for the Lord Jehovah is my strength and my song; he also is become my salvation.*

(See also Isa. 30:26, 40:1-2, 49:13, 51:3, 61:3, 66:13-14, Jer. 31:24-25, Zeph. 3:18-20)

12.   There will be a perfect administration of JUSTICE.

As previously mentioned, the Millennial Kingdom is not perfect, but we might say that it will near perfect. When there is an act of sin or crime, King Jesus will administer perfect justice in every case. No longer will wealth or fame sway the judicial system to one's favor. No longer will poverty or being from a minority bring undue or unfair punishment.

Isa. 9:7 - *Of the increase of his government and peace there shall be no end upon the throne of David, and upon his kingdom, to order it, and to establish it with judgment and with justice from henceforth even for ever. The zeal of the Lord of hosts will perform this.*

13.   There will be an unparalleled teaching ministry by the Holy Spirit so that earth's inhabitants will possess great KNOWLEDGE of the Lord.

At last, there is going to be ONE PERSON in charge of the whole planet and *everyone* will know Who He is and will bow to Him in obeisance. There won't be any struggling for the highest positions. Jesus will appoint everyone to their job.

Isa. 11:9 - *They shall not hurt nor destroy in all my holy mountain: for **the earth shall be full of the knowledge of the Lord**, as the waters cover the sea.*

(See also Isa. 11:1-2, 41:19-20, 54:13, Hab. 2:14)

14.   The original CURSE THAT WAS PLACED ON CREATION WILL BE REMOVED so the ground will give forth in great abundance. Also, nature will be changed to remove all of its fierceness and death.

As mentioned earlier, nature will flourish and agriculture will produce in great abundance. No longer will man have to toil and use artificial means (like fertilizer) to cause the earth to give forth of its great wealth of fruit, vegetables, flowers, and trees. And, in the animal kingdom, there will be no carnivores. All animals will be plant eaters. All viciousness of nature will be gone. All poisonous animals will become completely safe.

Isa. 11:6 - *The wolf also shall dwell with the lamb, and the leopard shall lie down with the kid; and the calf and the young lion and the fatling together; and a little child shall lead them.*
7   And the cow and the bear shall feed; their young ones shall lie down together; and the lion shall eat straw like the ox.
8   And the sucking child shall play on the hole of the asp, and the weaned child shall put his hand on the cockatrice' den.

(See also Isa. 65:25, Ezek. 34:25-28)

15.   Good health will prevail among the people and there will be NO SICKNESS and NO DEFORMITY.

No longer will there be birth defects or people with disabilities or all the various debilitating diseases. The blind, the lame, the deaf, the mentally handicapped and those suffering from cancer will be only a bad memory of the past. There will be no one ostracized because of their leprosy or other contagious disease. Everyone will have healthy bodies. There will no need for wheel chairs, seeing eye dogs, or prosthetics. Such things will be unheard of in that day.

Ezek. 34:16a - *I will seek that which was lost, and bring again that which was driven away, and will bind up that which was broken, and will strengthen that which was sick...*

Isa. 29:18 - *And in that day shall the deaf hear the words of the book, and the eyes of the blind shall see out of obscurity, and out of darkness.*

(See also Isa. 33:24, Jer. 30:17, Isa. 35:5, Zeph. 3:19)

16.   The Lord will STRENGTHEN THE WEAK and those who were persecuted and DEAL JUSTICE TO THOSE WHO WERE THE OPPRESSORS.

In the Millennial Kingdom, there will be no bullies or those who take advantage of those weaker than themselves.

Isa. 41:10 - *Fear thou not; for I am with thee: be not dismayed; for I am thy God: I will strengthen thee; yea, I will help thee; yea, I will uphold thee with the right hand of my righteousness.*

11 *Behold, all they that were incensed against thee shall be ashamed and confounded; they shall be as nothing; and they that strive with thee shall perish.*

(See also Isa. 42:6-7, 49:8-9, Zech. 9:11)

17. LONGEVITY of life will be restored to as it was in the days of Noah.

Isa. 65:20 - *There shall be no more thence an infant of days, nor an old man that hath not filled his days: for the child shall die a hundred years old; but the sinner being a hundred years old shall be accursed.*

Some have said that this scripture is saying that when a person reaches the age of 100 in the Millennial Kingdom, he will die if he has given his heart to Jesus. But that is totally without base.

Isaiah is simply pointing out that an "infant" will not die after only a few days of life. Nor will there be an "old man" who will die without reaching his full life span. And if a person should die at the age of 100, they would be considered a mere child. Only the accursed sinner will die that young.

The point of all these phrases is not about what age people will die, but about how long people will live! People will live 800, 900, 1000 years or longer in that time period, just as it was in the days of Noah before the flood. Thus,

18. There will be an enormous INCREASE IN HUMAN REPRODUCTION, so the earth's population will soar.

Although the Scriptures don't say this specifically, we would have to assume from this that families will be very large and that childbirth will be painless.

Deut. 28:4 - *Blessed shall be the fruit of thy body, and the fruit of the ground, and fruit of they cattle, the increase of thy kine, and the flocks of thy sheep.*

(See also Ezek. 47:22, Zech. 10:7-8)

19.   There will not be any idleness, but PEOPLE WILL LABOR under the supervision of the Lord to provide for all the needs of the kingdom. No one will steal the fruit of another's labor.

Unbelievable as it may seem to some, productive labor is necessary for happiness and satisfaction in the life of every human. God knew this, of course, when He created the perfect environment for Adam. Without responsibilities and productive labor, God knew that Adam would become bored, lazy, and unhappy. So, God gave him the job of naming all the animals and tending to the Garden of Eden (Gen. 2:15, 19).

Isa. 62:8 - *The Lord hath sworn by his right hand, and by the arm of his strength, Surely I will no more give thy corn to be meat for thine enemies; and the sons of the stranger shall not drink thy wine, **for the which thou hast labored;***
9   But they that have gathered it shall eat it, and praise the Lord; and they that have brought it together shall drink it in the courts of my holiness.

(See also Isa. 65:21-23)

20.   There will be an INCREASE IN LIGHT from both the sun and the moon. This may account for part of the increase in productivity of the earth.

This is not in the sense of an increase in the intensity of sunlight so that it burns and scorches the earth. This is an increase in the productive rays of the light spectrum that aids in plant growth.

Isa. 30:26 - *Moreover the light of the moon shall be as the light of the sun, and the light of the sun shall be sevenfold, as the light of seven days, in the day that the Lord bindeth up the breach of his people, and healeth the stroke of their wound.*

(See also Isa. 60:19-20)

21.   All the world will unite in SINGULAR WORSHIP of our Lord.

No more will there be many different religions or various denominations within a particular religion. There will only be one God, Jesus Christ, and all people will worship Him in unity, without dissention about what is the **right way** to worship Him.

Isa. 45:23 - *I have sworn by myself, the word is gone out of my mouth in righteousness, and shall not return, That unto me every knee shall bow, and every tongue shall swear.*

(See also Isa. 66:23, Zech. 13:2, 14:16, 8:23)

22.   There will be no more language barriers because everyone will speak the SAME LANGUAGE.

Zeph. 3:9 - *For then will I turn to the people a pure language, that they may all call upon the name of the Lord, to serve him with one consent.*

In a kind of pre-fulfillment of this prophecy, the Hebrew language was revived among the Jewish people by Eliezer Ben Yehuda in the early 20th century after becoming extinct as a national language for centuries. For many years, it was spoken only in the synagogue by those few rabbis who understood it and it was considered a "holy language" not for common communication. This, along with many other obstacles made it extremely difficult for Ben Yehuda to revive the ancient language. But he made it his life's goal and literally spent his life achieving it.

A fascinating book is written about Ben Yehuda's life:
Robert Saint John, *The Life Story of Ben Yehuda, Tongue of the Prophets*, (Balfour Books, 2013)

It can be found on Amazon.com

23. FELLOWSHIP WITH THE LORD will be in all its fullness as we bask in His divine presence.

We cannot imagine what a glorious day it will be when we actually live in the very presence of Jesus Christ! Nothing in all the world will compare to the overwhelming joy of being in His presence! To live for Him and to serve Him will be the greatest all blessings!

Ezek. 37:27 - *My tabernacle also shall be **with them**; yea, I will be their God, and they shall be my people.*

Zech. 2:10 - *Sing and rejoice, O daughter of Zion: for, lo, I come, and I will dwell in the midst of thee, saith the Lord.*
11 *And many nations shall be joined to the Lord in that day, and shall be my people: and I will dwell in the midst of thee, and thou shalt know that the Lord of hosts hath sent me unto thee.*
12 *And the Lord shall inherit Judah his portion in the holy land, and shall choose Jerusalem again.*
13 *Be silent, O all flesh, before the Lord; for he is raised up out of his holy habitation.*

But the Lord's beautiful earthly kingdom, in all of it goodness, will not be perfect because mortal humans who are still confined to their flesh will live there. Thus, the *"lust of the flesh, and the lust of the eyes, and the pride of life"* (I John 2:16) will still move people to commit sin. The thousand year kingdom, even with all of its good qualities, will end in **sinful failure** on the part of man.

At the end of the thousand years, Satan will be loosed for a short season to go into the world one last time and deceive the nations (Rev. 20:3, 7-9). He will stir up one final rebellion against Jesus. Those rebels will surround Jerusalem in an attempt to defeat the Lord, but God will send down fire from Heaven to devour them. Satan will then be thrown into the lake of fire to join the Antichrist and False Prophet where they will be *"tormented day and night for ever and ever."* (Rev. 20:10).

The Millennium
Quiz

1. The Second Coming of our Lord Jesus will occur at the _____ of the Tribulation period. At that time, He will defeat the Antichrist, destroy the enemies of God, and judge the mortals of earth in a judgment that we usually call The _____ of _____.

2. This earthly judgment will take place in the Valley of _____.

3. King Jesus will then establish His earthly kingdom, called the Millennial Kingdom, for a period of _____ years.

4. The Bible teaches that we Christians of the Church Age will receive our immortal bodies at the Rapture and that during the Millennium, we will _____ with Christ over the mortals on earth.

5. Satan will be _____ (killed, exiled to outer space, locked up) during the Millennium.

6. T or F - The Millennial Kingdom will be a perfect time when all sin will be abolished.

7. The overall character of the Millennial Kingdom will be that it is a time of _____, _____, and _____.

8. Longevity will be as it was in the days of _____.

9. During the Millennium, weapons of war will be converted to tools of _____ because there will be no wars or militaries.

10. At the end of the Millennium, Satan will be _____ for a season to go into the world and _____ the nations for one final rebellion against Jesus and His kingdom.

11. At that time, Satan will be thrown into ____ _____ of _____, which will be his eternal abode.

12. After the Millennium, God will make a new Heaven and a new earth and we, the saints of God, will live eternally in a new city on earth called The New _____.

The Millennium
Quiz Answers

1. end, Judgment of Nations

2. Jehoshaphat (Joel 3:1-2)

3. 1000

4. reign

5. locked up (in that special place of imprisonment for spirits called the Bottomless Pit, or the Abyss)

6. False (Mortals will still deal with the sin of the flesh… greed, lust, etc.)

7. peace, justice, righteousness

8. Noah

9. agriculture

10. loosed, deceive

11. The Lake of Fire

12. Jerusalem

Made in the USA
San Bernardino, CA
31 December 2014